*Opposing Viewpoints*®

# Other Books of Related Interest

*Opposing Viewpoints Series*

Abortion
American Values
America's Children
America's Future
America's Prisons
America's Victims
Child Abuse
Crime and Criminals
Criminal Justice
Culture Wars
Death and Dying
Gangs
The Homeless
Interracial America
Juvenile Justice
The Legal System
Mental Illness
Race Relations
Suicide
21st Century Earth
Violence
War on Drugs

*Current Controversies Series*

The Abortion Controversy
Drug Trafficking
Ethics
Family Violence
Gun Control
Hate Crimes
Police Brutality
Urban Terrorism
Violence Against Women
Youth Violence

*At Issue Series*

Domestic Violence
Policing the Police

# The DEATH PENALTY
## *Opposing Viewpoints*®

David Bender & Bruno Leone, *Series Editors*

Paul A. Winters, *Book Editor*

OPPOSING
VIEWPOINTS®
SERIES

Greenhaven Press, Inc., San Diego, CA

Greenhaven Press, Inc.
PO Box 289009
San Diego, CA 92198-9009


Library of Congress Cataloging-in-Publication Data

The death penalty : opposing viewpoints / Paul A. Winters, book editor.
    p.    cm. — (Opposing viewpoints series)
  Includes bibliographical references and index.
  ISBN 1-56510-510-9 (lib. : alk. paper). — ISBN 1-56510-509-5 (pbk. : alk. paper)
  1. Capital punishment. I. Winters, Paul A., 1965–    .
II. Series: Opposing viewpoints series (Unnumbered)
HV8694.D385    1997
364.6′6—dc20                                               96-22575
                                                               CIP


Third Edition Revised
Copyright © 1986, 1991, 1997 by Greenhaven Press, Inc.
Printed in the U.S.A.

"Congress shall make no law . . . abridging the freedom of speech, or of the press."

First Amendment to the U.S. Constitution

The basic foundation of our democracy is the First Amendment guarantee of freedom of expression. The Opposing Viewpoints Series is dedicated to the concept of this basic freedom and the idea that it is more important to practice it than to enshrine it.

# Contents

# Why Consider Opposing Viewpoints?

*"The only way in which a human being can make some approach to knowing the whole of a subject is by hearing what can be said about it by persons of every variety of opinion and studying all modes in which it can be looked at by every character of mind. No wise man ever acquired his wisdom in any mode but this."*

John Stuart Mill

In our media-intensive culture it is not difficult to find differing opinions. Thousands of newspapers and magazines and dozens of radio and television talk shows resound with differing points of view. The difficulty lies in deciding which opinion to agree with and which "experts" seem the most credible. The more inundated we become with differing opinions and claims, the more essential it is to hone critical reading and thinking skills to evaluate these ideas. Opposing Viewpoints books address this problem directly by presenting stimulating debates that can be used to enhance and teach these skills. The varied opinions contained in each book examine many different aspects of a single issue. While examining these conveniently edited opposing views, readers can develop critical thinking skills such as the ability to compare and contrast authors' credibility, facts, argumentation styles, use of persuasive techniques, and other stylistic tools. In short, the Opposing Viewpoints Series is an ideal way to attain the higher-level thinking and reading skills so essential in a culture of diverse and contradictory opinions.

In addition to providing a tool for critical thinking, Opposing Viewpoints books challenge readers to question their own strongly held opinions and assumptions. Most people form their opinions on the basis of upbringing, peer pressure, and personal, cultural, or professional bias. By reading carefully balanced opposing views, readers must directly confront new ideas as well as the opinions of those with whom they disagree. This is not to simplistically argue that everyone who reads opposing views will—or should—change his or her opinion. Instead, the series enhances readers' depth of understanding of their own views by encouraging confrontation with opposing ideas. Careful examination of others' views can lead to the readers' understanding of the logical inconsistencies in their own opinions, perspective on why they hold an opinion, and the consideration of the possibility that their opinion requires further evaluation.

## Evaluating Other Opinions

To ensure that this type of examination occurs, Opposing Viewpoints books present all types of opinions. Prominent spokespeople on different sides of each issue as well as well-known professionals from many disciplines challenge the reader. An additional goal of the series is to provide a forum for other, less known, or even unpopular viewpoints. The opinion of an ordinary person who has had to make the decision to cut off life support from a terminally ill relative, for example, may be just as valuable and provide just as much insight as a medical ethicist's professional opinion. The editors have two additional purposes in including these less known views. One, the editors encourage readers to respect others' opinions—even when not enhanced by professional credibility. It is only by reading or listening to and objectively evaluating others' ideas that one can determine whether they are worthy of consideration. Two, the inclusion of such viewpoints encourages the important critical thinking skill of objectively evaluating an author's credentials and bias. This evaluation will illuminate an author's reasons for taking a particular stance on an issue and will aid in readers' evaluation of the author's ideas.

As series editors of the Opposing Viewpoints Series, it is our hope that these books will give readers a deeper understanding of the issues debated and an appreciation of the complexity of even seemingly simple issues when good and honest people disagree. This awareness is particularly important in a democratic society such as ours in which people enter into public debate to determine the common good. Those with whom one disagrees should not be regarded as enemies but rather as people whose views deserve careful examination and may shed light on one's own.

Thomas Jefferson once said that "difference of opinion leads to inquiry, and inquiry to truth." Jefferson, a broadly educated man, argued that "if a nation expects to be ignorant and free . . . it expects what never was and never will be." As individuals and as a nation, it is imperative that we consider the opinions of others and examine them with skill and discernment. The Opposing Viewpoints Series is intended to help readers achieve this goal.

David L. Bender & Bruno Leone,
Series Editors

# Introduction

*"I feel morally and intellectually obligated simply to concede that the death penalty experiment has failed."*

Harry A. Blackmun

*"The death penalty is not one of the 'cruel and unusual punishments' prohibited by the Eighth Amendment."*

Antonin Scalia

In February 1994, two months before his retirement from the Supreme Court, Justice Harry A. Blackmun articulated his personal conviction that capital punishment in the United States is not applied fairly and consistently and is therefore unconstitutional. In response, Justice Antonin Scalia reproached Blackmun for interpreting the Constitution according to personal convictions. The disagreement between the justices revisited arguments presented in the 1972 Supreme Court decision in the case of *Furman v. Georgia*. That 5-4 ruling adjudged the death penalty to be unconstitutional as practiced at the time because its arbitrary application by juries violated the Eighth Amendment's ban on cruel and unusual punishment.

The *Furman v. Georgia* decision was a collection of three capital cases in which black defendants received death sentences for the murder or rape of white victims. In defense of the three convicted men, lawyers put forward two main arguments for the abolition of the death penalty, according to David Von Drehle, a *Washington Post* reporter and author of *Among the Lowest of the Dead: A Decade on Death Row*. First, the lawyers asserted that capital sentences were imposed arbitrarily. For example, they argued, two of the *Furman* defendants were sentenced to death for rape, whereas some murderers received sentences of life imprisonment or less. Second, they contended that sentences of death were carried out so infrequently that they did not serve as an effective deterrent.

Although five justices voted to strike down the death penalty as a violation of the Eighth Amendment, they cited very different reasons for doing so, according to Von Drehle. Justices William J. Brennan and Thurgood Marshall believed that capital punishment was morally unacceptable and held that it should be banned. William O. Douglas and Potter Stewart asserted that death sentences were cruel and unusual because they were inflicted by juries in an arbitrary and capricious manner—being sentenced to death was as random as being struck by lightning, in Stewart's opinion. Without objective standards to limit the death penalty to the worst crimes, Stewart and Douglas reasoned, juries were free to apply it in a way that was biased and unfair. On the other hand, although he favored use of the death penalty, Justice Byron White maintained that it was cruel and unusual because the sentences were not handed out consistently. In his written opinion, he implied that too many murderers escaped the death penalty because juries were free not to impose it.

*Furman* effectively struck down all existing state and federal capital punishment statutes. In response, thirty-five states quickly wrote new capital punishment statutes that attempted to meet the requirements for fairness and consistency established by the Court. According to Wendy Kaminer, author of *It's All the Rage: Crime and Culture*, states had two alternatives: They could respond to the arguments of Douglas and Stewart or they could follow the advice contained in White's opinion. Some states wrote laws that attempted to guide the discretion of juries in the application of the death penalty; other states wrote laws that made the death penalty the mandatory punishment for murder. In 1976, these new laws came before the Supreme Court. In the decision of *Gregg v. Georgia*, the Court upheld the guided discretion sentencing statutes but struck down the mandatory death penalties. The justices held that although mandatory penalties provided consistency in sentencing, they were unconstitutional because they did not allow juries to take into consideration mitigating factors about the criminal or the crime. In effect, mandatory sentences were struck down because they prevented juries from extending mercy to individuals deemed worthy. The guided discretion statutes were upheld because they instructed juries to weigh aggravating and mitigating factors in a crime and to determine a fair punishment based on these considerations.

Since 1976, the Supreme Court has issued many decisions clarifying the role that mitigating and aggravating factors should play in capital cases. However, Justice Blackmun concluded in 1994 that despite this effort, the death penalty is still administered in an arbitrary manner in violation of the Eighth Amendment and therefore should be struck down once again. The power to extend mercy guaranteed to juries in the *Gregg* decision can be applied arbitrarily, he argues, and fundamentally contradicts the goal of consistency established by the *Furman* ruling. In order for the death penalty to be applied consistently, he reasons, the jury's power to extend mercy would have to be limited. The constitutional requirements of fairness and consistency are therefore "irreconcilable in the context of capital punishment," Blackmun concludes, since every "step toward consistency is a step away from fairness."

Although he agrees that the contradiction between fairness and consistency exists, Justice Antonin Scalia replies that the language of the Constitution "clearly permits the death penalty to be imposed" and that capital punishment therefore cannot be unconstitutional. He finds fault with the Court decisions that established contradictory goals rather than with the death penalty itself. In other cases, Scalia has maintained that the jury's power not to impose the death sentence can and should be limited. Justice Clarence Thomas, agreeing that capital punishment is constitutional, argues that states have been successful in balancing the requirements of fairness and consistency established in *Furman* and *Gregg*. He asserts that "if the death penalty is constitutional, states must surely be able to administer it pursuant to rational procedures that comport with the Eighth Amendment's most basic requirements."

The issues raised in the 1972 Supreme Court case *Furman v. Georgia*—whether execution is a "cruel and unusual punishment," whether death sentences are handed out fairly or discriminatorily, and whether capital punishment is an effective deterrent—have been debated for centuries. The first chapter of *Death Penalty: Opposing Viewpoints* examines historical writings on the subject. Following chapters explore contemporary views on these questions: Is the Death Penalty Just? Is the Death Penalty an Effective Punishment? Is the Death Penalty Applied Unfairly? In this anthology, authors examine and debate the persisting issues surrounding sentences of death.

# Three Centuries of Debate on the Death Penalty

# Chapter Preface

Controversy over the death penalty is recent in the history of humankind. Most ancient societies accepted the idea that certain crimes deserved capital punishment. Ancient Roman and Mosaic law endorsed the notion of retaliation; they believed in the rule of "an eye for an eye." Similarly, the ancient Egyptians, Assyrians, and Greeks all executed citizens for a variety of offenses, ranging from perjury to murder.

Adherence to the death penalty continued into the Middle Ages, during which religious crimes such as sacrilege, heresy, and atheism were punishable by death. European settlers brought the death penalty to the American colonies, where idolatry, witchcraft, blasphemy, murder, sodomy, adultery, rape, perjury, and rebellion were all capital crimes in 1636. This continuing use of the death penalty reflected society's belief that severe crimes warranted severe punishments and that such punishments would deter others from committing such crimes.

This view was challenged during the Enlightenment of the eighteenth century, which dramatically altered European and American perceptions about political and social issues such as capital punishment. A movement to abolish or at least restrict the death penalty began to take shape in the writings of Cesare Beccaria, Montesquieu, Voltaire, and others. Their views were reflected in the words of American revolutionary Benjamin Rush in 1792: "The punishment of murder by death is contrary to reason, and to the order and happiness of society." Some European leaders banned the death penalty. One such leader, Catherine the Great of Russia, stated, "There can be no necessity for taking away the life of a citizen."

Other philosophers of this period, however, defended the death penalty. German philosopher Immanuel Kant asserted that the death penalty was the most equitable punishment for murder. Unremorseful murderers deserve to die, he believed, while remorseful, guilt-ridden murderers would welcome death as a relief from their emotional pain. The United States and most European nations continued to execute criminals, believing in its justness and in its deterrent effect.

Eighteenth-century philosophers such as Kant and Beccaria sparked a controversy that continued into the nineteenth and twentieth centuries. The following chapter presents a variety of historical arguments supporting and opposing the death penalty.

*"Those who shew no mercy should find none;
and if Hanging will not restrain them, Hanging
them in Chains, and Starving them, or . . .
breaking them on the Wheel . . . should."*

# The Death Penalty Will Discourage Crime (1701)

Paper Presented Before the English Parliament

In eighteenth-century England, some two hundred crimes were punishable by death, including pickpocketing and petty theft. Many people were attempting to reform this excess of executions by reducing the sentences for many offenses. Others believed, however, that the death penalty should continue to be rigorously applied for heinous crimes. In the following viewpoint, the author states that punishments should remain severe and perhaps be even more so. He argues that keeping the death penalty a very real threat is the only way to stop people from committing violent and offensive crimes.

As you read, consider the following questions:

1. Why does the author believe the death penalty must be used "steadily and impartially"?
2. On what does the author base his argument that there should be differences in the degrees of punishments?
3. What does the author say society should be careful of when applying the death penalty?

*Hanging Not Punishment Enough for Murtherers, Highway Men, and House-Breakers.* London: A. Balwin, 1701.

I am sensible, That the *English* Clemency and Mildness appear eminently in our Laws and Constitutions; but since it is found that *Ill* Men are grown so much more incorrigible, than in our fore-fathers Days, is it not fit that *Good* Men should grow less merciful to them, since gentler Methods are ineffectual?

I acknowledge also, That the Spirit of Christianity disposes us to Patience and Forbearance, insomuch that when the *Roman* Emperors began to grow Christian, we are informed, That most Capital Punishments were taken away, and turned into others less Sanguinary; either that they might have longer time for Repentance, (an Indulgence agreeable to the Zeal and Piety of those Good Ages) or that the length and continuance of their Punishment might be more Exemplary. And I acknowledge with the Wise *Quintilian, That if Ill men could be made Good, as, it must be granted, they sometimes may, it is for the Interest of the Commonwealth, that they should rather be spared than punished.* And I know, that 'tis frequently alledg'd, That you take away a Better thing, and that is a Man's Life, for that which is worse, and that is, your Money and Goods; but tho' this be speciously enough urged, yet I doubt not, but the Publick Safety and Happiness may lawfully and reasonably be secured by this way, if it can by no other. . . .

## Show No Mercy to the Merciless

I must beg leave to say, that those who shew no mercy should find none; and if Hanging will not restrain them, Hanging them in Chains, and Starving them, or (if Murtherers and Robbers at the same time, or Night incendiaries) breaking them on the Wheel, or Whipping them to Death, a *Roman* Punishment should.

I know that Torments so unusual and unknown to us may at first surprize us, and appear unreasonable; but I hope easily to get over that difficulty, and make it appear upon Examination, that *that* will be the more probable way to secure us from our fears of them, and the means of preserving great numbers of them, who now yearly by an easie Death are taken off at the Gallows. For to Men so far corrupted in their Principles and Practices, and that have no expectations beyond the Grave (for such, I fear, is the case of most of them) no Argument will be so cogent, as Pain in an intense degree; and a few such Examples made, will be so terrifying, that I persuade myself it would be a Law but seldom put in Execution.

## The Death Penalty Must Be Used

But then I must add, that I fear it will not have its due effects, if it be too often dispens'd with; since *that* will be apt to give ground to every Offender, to hope he may be of the number of *those*, who shall escape, and so the good end of the Law will be defeated. For if Favour or Affection, or a Man's being of a good

Family, or Money can prevail, and take off the Penalty of the Statute; if it be not executed steadily and impartially, with an exact hand (still giving allowance for extraordinary Cases) it will serve to little purpose, since many will be found (as ill men easily flatter themselves) who will not fear a Law, that has sharp Teeth indeed, but does but sometimes bite. And this, I believe, must be allowed to be the only way to root out our Native Enemies, as they truly are; as might lately have been seen in a Neighbouring Kingdom, where severity, without the least mixture of mercy, did so sweep High-way Men out of the Nation, that it has been confidently said, that a Man might some time since have *openly* carried his Money without fear of losing it. That he cannot *now*, is to be charged upon their great numbers of Soldiers, without Employment and Plunder, and in poor pitiful Pay; and, it may be, on the very great necessities of the People, and make 'em desperate and careless of their Lives.

## Severe Penalties Prevent Crime

In England, Germany, and France, a man knows, that if he commit murder, every person around him will, from that instant, become his enemy, and use every means to seize him and bring him to justice. He knows that he will be immediately carried to prison, and put to an ignominious death, amidst the execrations of his countrymen. Impressed with these sentiments, and with the natural horror for murder which such sentiments augment, the populace of those countries hardly ever have recourse to stabbing in their accidental quarrels, however they may be inflamed with anger and rage. The lowest black-guard in the streets of London will not draw a knife against an antagonist far superior to himself in strength. He will fight him fairly with his fists as long as he can, and bear the severest drubbing, rather than use a means of defence which is held in detestation by his countrymen, and which would bring him to the gallows.

John Moore, *The Opinions of Different Authors upon the Punishment of Death*, 1812.

'Tis a Rule in Civil Law, and Reason, *That the Punishment should not exceed the fault*. If Death then be due to a Man, who surreptitiously steals the Value of Five Shillings (as it is made by a late Statute) surely *He* who puts me in fear of my Life, and breaks the King's Peace, and it may be, murthers me at last, and burns my House, deserves another sort of Censure; and if the one must die, the other should be made to *feel himself die. . . .*

The frequent Repetitions of the same Crimes, even in defiance of the present Laws in being, is a just ground of enacting somewhat more terrible; and indeed seems to challenge and require it.

Farther still; at the *last great day* doubtless there will be degrees of Torment, proportionable to Mens guilt and sin here; and I can see no reason why we may not imitate the Divine justice, and inflict an Animadversion suitable to such enormous Offenders.

And this, I am persuaded, will best answer the End of Sanguinary Laws, which are not *chiefly* intended to punish the present Criminal, but to hinder others from being so; and on that account Punishments in the Learned Languages are called *Examples*, as being design'd to be such to all mankind. . . .

## Careful of Shedding Human Blood

Still I am sensible, that tho' I argue for severity, in general ought to be tender of shedding human blood; For *there is such a Consanguinity and Relation between all mankind that no one ought to hurt another, unless for some good end to be obtain'd.* And *Bodily Punishment,* as the Civilian well observes, *is greater than any Pecuniary mulcts*; and every Man knows that he who loses his Life, is a much greater sufferer than he whose Goods are confiscated, or is Fined in the most unreasonable manner in the World.

But my design is not, that Man's blood *should* be shed, but that it should *not*; and I verily believe, that for *Five* Men Condemned and Executed *now*, you would hardly have *one then*. For those Men out of Terror of such a Law, would ('tis to be hoped) either apply themselves to honest Labour and Industry; or else would remove to our *Plantations*, where they are wanted, and so many useful Hands would not be yearly lost.

But I must add, That *it is not fit, that men in Criminal Causes,* as the Civil Law well directs, *should be condemned, unless the Evidence be clearer than the mid-day Sun*; and no Man should expire in such horrid Agonies, for whose Innocence there is the least pretense.

*"The punishment of death has never prevented determined men from injuring society."*

# The Death Penalty Will Not Discourage Crime (1764)

Cesare Beccaria

An Italian criminologist, Cesare Beccaria lived and died in the 1700s. He influenced local economic reforms and stimulated penal reform throughout Europe. In 1764 he published *An Essay on Crimes and Punishments*, one of the first arguments against capital punishment and inhumane treatment of criminals. In the following viewpoint, Beccaria condemns capital punishment on several grounds, including that it is not a deterrent to crime and is irrevocable.

As you read, consider the following questions:

1. Why does Beccaria believe that the death penalty may be justified if a man is a threat to government?
2. What does an execution inspire in others, according to the author? What does he say about this reaction?
3. What does Beccaria say about life imprisonment?

Cesare Beccaria, *An Essay on Crimes and Punishments*, originally published in London by F. Newberry, 1775.

The useless profusion of punishments, which has never made men better, induces me to enquire, whether the punishment of *death* be really just or useful in a well governed state? What *right*, I ask, have men to cut the throats of their fellow-creatures? Certainly not that on which the sovereignty and laws are founded. The laws, as I have said before, are only the sum of the smallest portions of the private liberty of each individual, and represent the general will, which is the aggregate of that of each individual. Did any one ever give to others the right of taking away his life? Is it possible, that in the smallest portions of the liberty of each, sacrificed to the good of the public, can be contained the greatest of all good, life? If it were so, how shall it be reconciled to the maxim which tells us, that a man has no right to kill himself? Which he certainly must have, if he could give it away to another.

But the punishment of death is not authorized by any right; for I have demonstrated that no such right exists. It is therefore a war of a whole nation against a citizen, whose destruction they consider as necessary, or useful to the general good. But if I can further demonstrate, that it is neither necessary nor useful, I shall have gained the cause of humanity.

## Only One Reason for the Death Penalty

The death of a citizen cannot be necessary, but in one case. When, though deprived of his liberty, he has such power and connections as may endanger the security of the nation; when his existence may produce a dangerous revolution in the established form of government. But even in this case, it can only be necessary when a nation is on the verge of recovering or losing its liberty; or in times of absolute anarchy, when the disorders themselves hold the place of laws. But in a reign of tranquillity; in a form of government approved by the united wishes of the nation; in a state well fortified from enemies without, and supported by strength within, and opinion, perhaps more efficacious; where all power is lodged in the hands of a true sovereign; where riches can purchase pleasures and not authority, there can be no necessity for taking away the life of a subject.

If the experience of all ages be not sufficient to prove, that the punishment of death has never prevented determined men from injuring society; if the example of the Romans; if twenty years reign of Elizabeth, empress of Russia, in which she gave the fathers of their country an example more illustrious than many conquests bought with blood; if, I say, all this be not sufficient to persuade mankind, who always suspect the voice of reason, and who choose rather to be led by authority, let us consult human nature in proof of my assertion.

It is not the intenseness of the pain that has the greatest effect on the mind, but its continuance; for our sensibility is more easily and more powerfully affected by weak but repeated impressions, than by a violent, but momentary, impulse. The power of habits is universal over every sensible being. As it is by that we learn to speak, to walk, and to satisfy our necessities, so the ideas of morality are stamped on our minds by repeated impressions. The death of a criminal is a terrible but momentary spectacle, and therefore a less efficacious method of deterring others, than the continued example of a man deprived of his liberty, condemned, as a beast of burthen, to repair, by his labour, the injury he has done to society. *If I commit such a crime*, says the spectator to himself, *I shall be reduced to that miserable condition for the rest of my life.* A much more powerful preventive than the fear of death, which men always behold in distant obscurity.

## A Dead Man Is Good for Nothing

It hath long since been observed, that a man after he is hanged is good for nothing, and that punishment invented for the good of society, ought to be useful to society. It is evident, that a score of stout robbers, condemned for life to some public work, would serve the state in their punishment, and that hanging them is a benefit to nobody but the executioner.

*Commentary on Cesare Beccaria*, attributed to Voltaire, c. 1770.

The terrors of death make so slight an impression, that it has not force enough to withstand the forgetfulness natural to mankind, even in the most essential things; especially when assisted by the passions. Violent impressions surprise us, but their effect is momentary; they are fit to produce those revolutions which instantly transform a common man into a Lacedaemonian or a Persian; but in a free and quiet government they ought to be rather frequent than strong.

The execution of a criminal is, to the multitude, a spectacle, which in some excites compassion mixed with indignation. These sentiments occupy the mind much more than that salutary terror which the laws endeavour to inspire; but in the contemplation of continued suffering, terror is the only, or a least predominant sensation. The severity of a punishment should be just sufficient to excite compassion in the spectators, as it is intended more for them than for the criminal.

A punishment, to be just, should have only that degree of severity which is sufficient to deter others. Now there is no man, who upon the least reflection, would put in competition total and perpetual loss of his liberty, with the greatest advantages he could possibly obtain in consequence of a crime. Perpetual slavery, then, has in it all that is necessary to deter the most hardened and determined, as much as the punishment of death. I say it has more. There are many who can look upon death with intrepidity and firmness; some through fanaticism, and others through vanity, which attends us even to the grave; others from a desperate resolution, either to get rid of their misery, or cease to live: but fanaticism and vanity forsake the criminal in slavery, in chains and fetters, in an iron cage; and despair seems rather the beginning than the end of their misery. The mind, by collecting itself and uniting all its force, can, for a moment, repel assailing grief; but its most vigorous efforts are insufficient to resist perpetual wretchedness.

In all nations, where death is used as a punishment, every example supposes a new crime committed. Whereas in perpetual slavery, every criminal affords a frequent and lasting example; and if it be necessary that men should often be witnesses of the power of the laws, criminals should often be put to death; but this supposes a frequency of crimes; and from hence this punishment will cease to have its effect, so that it must be useful and useless at the same time.

## Slavery and the Death Penalty

I shall be told, that perpetual slavery is as painful a punishment as death, and therefore as cruel. I answer, that if all the miserable moments in the life of a slave were collected into one point, it would be a more cruel punishment than any other; but these are scattered through his whole life, whilst the pain of death exerts all its force in a moment. There is also another advantage in the punishment of slavery, which is, that it is more terrible to the spectator than to the sufferer himself; for the spectator considers the sum of all his wretched moments, whilst the sufferer, by the misery of the present, is prevented from thinking of the future. All evils are increased by the imagination, and the sufferer finds resources and consolations, of which the spectators are ignorant; who judge by their own sensibility of what passes in a mind, by habit grown callous to misfortune.

Let us, for a moment, attend to the reasoning of a robber or assassin, who is deterred from violating the laws by the gibbet or the wheel. I am sensible, that to develop the sentiments of one's own heart, is an art which education only can teach: but although a villain may not be able to give a clear account of his principles, they nevertheless influence his conduct. He reasons thus:

> What are these laws, that I am bound to respect, which make so great a difference between me and the rich man? He refuses me the farthing I ask of him, and excuses himself, by

bidding me have recourse to labour with which he is unacquainted. Who made these laws? The rich and the great, who never deigned to visit the miserable hut of the poor; who have never seen him dividing a piece of mouldly bread, amidst the cries of his famished children and the tears of his wife. Let us break those ties, fatal to the greatest part of mankind, and only useful to a few indolent tyrants. Let us attack injustice at its source. I will return to my natural state of independence. I shall live free and happy on the fruits of my courage and industry. A day of pain and repentance may come, but it will be short; and for an hour of grief I shall enjoy years of pleasure and liberty. King of a small number, as determined as myself, I will correct the mistakes of fortune; and I shall see those tyrants grow pale and tremble at the sight of him, whom, with insulting pride, they would not suffer to rank with their dogs and horses.

Religion then presents itself to the mind of this lawless villain, and promising him almost a certainty of eternal happiness upon the easy terms of repentance, contributes much to lessen the horror of the last scene of the tragedy.

---

### Horrible Punishments Serve No Purpose

A government that persists in retaining these horrible punishments can only assign one reason in justification of their conduct: that they have already so degraded and brutalized the habits of the people, that they cannot be restrained by any moderate punishments.

Are more atrocities committed in those countries where such punishments are unknown? Certainly not: the most savage banditti are always to be found under laws the most severe, and it is no more than what might be expected. The fate with which they are threatened hardens them to the sufferings of others as well as to their own. They know that they can expect no lenity, and they consider their acts of cruelty as retaliations.

Jeremy Bentham, *The Opinions of Different Authors on the Punishment of Death*, 1809.

---

But he who foresees, that he must pass a great number of years, even his whole life, in pain and slavery; a slave to those laws by which he was protected; in sight of his fellow citizens, with whom he lives in freedom and society; makes an useful comparison between those evils, the uncertainty of his success, and the shortness of the time in which he shall enjoy the fruits of his transgression. The example of those wretches continually before his eyes, make a much greater impression on him than a punishment, which, instead of correcting, makes him more obdurate.

The punishment of death is pernicious to society, from the example of barbarity it affords. If the passions, or the necessity of war, have taught men to shed the blood of their fellow creatures, the laws, which are intended to moderate the ferocity of mankind, should not increase it by examples of barbarity, the more horrible, as this punishment is usually attended with formal pageantry. Is it not absurd, that the laws, which detest and punish homicide, should, in order to prevent murder, publicly commit murder themselves? . . .

## Seeking Truth

If it be objected, that almost all the nations in all ages have punished certain crimes with death, I answer, that the force of these examples vanishes, when opposed to truth, against which prescription is urged in vain. The history of mankind is an immense sea of errors, in which a few obscure truths may here and there be found.

But human sacrifices have also been common in almost all nations. That some societies only, either few in number, or for a very short time, abstained from the punishment of death, is rather favourable to my argument, for such is the fate of great truths, that their duration is only as a flash of lightning in the long and dark night of error. The happy time is not yet arrived, when truth, as falsehood has been hitherto, shall be the portion of the greatest number.

*"We show . . . our regard for [human life] by the adoption of a rule that he who violates that right in another forfeits it for himself."*

# Society Must Retain the Death Penalty for Murder (1868)

John Stuart Mill

John Stuart Mill, prominent philosopher and economist, is probably best known as the author of the famous essay *On Liberty*. From 1865 to 1868 he served as a member of the British Parliament and constantly advocated political and social reforms such as emancipation for women, and the development of labor organizations and farm cooperatives. In the following viewpoint, taken from a Parliamentary Debate on April 21, 1868, Mill argues that while he is an advocate for lesser penalties for crimes such as theft, society must retain the death penalty for crimes of murder.

As you read, consider the following questions:

1. Why does the author argue that the death penalty is the most humane alternative for the criminal?
2. Does the death penalty deter crime, according to Mill?
3. Why does the author say he disagrees with the philanthropists on the issue of the death penalty?

John Stuart Mill, *Hansard's Parliamentary Debate,* 3rd Series, London: April 21, 1868.

It is always a matter of regret to me to find myself, on a public question, opposed to those who are called—sometimes in the way of honour, and sometimes in what is intended for ridicule—the philanthropists. Of all persons who take part in public affairs, they are those for whom, on the whole, I feel the greatest amount of respect; for their characteristic is, that they devote their time, their labour, and much of their money to objects purely public, with a less admixture of either personal or class selfishness, than any other class of politicians whatever. On almost all the great questions, scarcely any politicians are so steadily and almost uniformly to be found on the side of right; and they seldom err, but by an exaggerated application of some just and highly important principle. On the very subject that is now occupying us we all know what signal service they have rendered. It is through their efforts that our criminal laws . . . have so greatly relaxed their most revolting and most impolitic ferocity, that aggravated murder is now practically the only crime which is punished with death by any of our lawful tribunals; and we are even now deliberating whether the extreme penalty should be retained in that solitary case. This vast gain, not only to humanity, but to the ends of penal justice, we owe to the philanthropists; and if they are mistaken, as I cannot but think they are, in the present instance, it is only in not perceiving the right time and place for stopping in a career hitherto so eminently beneficial. Sir, there is a point at which, I conceive, that career ought to stop.

## Just Penalty for Some Circumstances

When there has been brought home to any one, by conclusive evidence, the greatest crime known to the law; and when the attendant circumstances suggest no palliation of the guilt, no hope that the culprit may even yet not be unworthy to live among mankind, nothing to make it probable that the crime was an exception to his general character rather than a consequence of it, then I confess it appears to me that to deprive the criminal of the life of which he has proved himself to be unworthy—solemnly to blot him out from the fellowship of mankind and from the catalogue of the living—is the most appropriate, as it is certainly the most impressive, mode in which society can attach to so great a crime the penal consequences which for the security of life it is indispensable to annex to it. I defend this penalty, when confined to atrocious cases, on the very ground on which it is commonly attacked—on that of humanity to the criminal; as beyond comparison the least cruel mode in which it is possible adequately to deter from the crime. If, in our horror of inflicting death, we endeavour to devise some punishment for the living criminal which shall act on the human mind with a deterrent force at all comparable to that of death, we are driven to inflictions less severe indeed in appearance, and therefore less efficacious, but far more cruel in reality.

## The Most Powerful Deterrent

The punishment of death is unquestionably the most powerful deterrent, the most effective preventive, that can be applied. Human nature teaches this fact. An instinct that outruns all reasoning, a dreadful horror that overcomes all other sentiments, works in us all when we contemplate it.

Samuel Hand, *The North American Review*, December 1881.

Few, I think, would venture to propose, as a punishment for aggravated murder, less than imprisonment with hard labour for life; that is the fate to which a murderer would be consigned by the mercy which shrinks from putting him to death. But has it been sufficiently considered what sort of a mercy this is, and what kind of life it leaves to him? If, indeed, the punishment is not really inflicted—if it becomes the sham which a few years ago such punishments were rapidly becoming—then, indeed, its adoption would be almost tantamount to giving up the attempt to repress murder altogether. But if it really is what it professes to be, and if it is realized in all its rigour by the popular imagination, as it very probably would not be, but as it must be if it is to be efficacious, it will be so shocking that when the memory of the crime is no longer fresh, there will be almost insuperable difficulty in executing it. What comparison can there really be, in point of severity, between consigning a man to the short pang of a rapid death, and immuring him in a living tomb, there to linger out what may be a long life in the hardest and most monotonous toil, without any of its alleviations or rewards—debarred from all pleasant sights and sounds, and cut off from all earthly hope, except a slight mitigation of bodily restraint, or a small improvement of diet? Yet even such a lot as this, because there is no one moment at which the suffering is of terrifying intensity, and, above all, because it does not contain the element, so imposing to the imagination, of the unknown, is universally reputed a milder punishment than death—stands in all codes as a mitigation of the capital penalty, and is thankfully accepted as such. For it is characteristic of all punishments which depend on duration for their efficacy—all, therefore, which are not corporal or pecuniary—that they are more rigorous than they seem; while it is, on the contrary, one of the strongest recommendations a punishment can have, that it should seem more rigorous than it is; for its practical power depends far less on what it is than on what it seems.

There is not, I should think, any human infliction which makes an impression on the imagination so entirely out of proportion to its real severity as the punishment of death. The punishment must be mild indeed which does not add more to the sum of human misery than is necessarily or directly added by the execution of a criminal. . . . The most that human laws can do to anyone in the matter of death is to hasten it; the man would have died at any rate; not so very much later, and on the average, I fear, with a considerably greater amount of bodily suffering. Society is asked, then, to denude itself of an instrument of punishment which, in the grave cases to which alone it is suitable, effects its purpose at a less cost of human suffering than any other; which, while it inspires more terror, is less cruel in actual fact than any punishment that we should think of substituting for it. My hon. Friend [Mr. Gilpin] says that it does not inspire terror, and that experience proves it to be a failure. But the influence of a punishment is not to be estimated by its effect on hardened criminals. Those whose habitual way of life keeps them, so to speak, at all times within sight of the gallows, do grow to care less about it;  as, to compare good things with bad, an old soldier is not much affected by the chance of dying in battle. I can afford to admit all that is often said about the indifference of professional criminals to the gallows. Though of that indifference one-third is probably bravado and another third confidence that they shall have the luck to escape, it is quite probable that the remaining third is real. But the efficacy of a punishment which acts principally through the imagination, is chiefly to be measured by the impression it makes on those who are still innocent: by the horror with which it surrounds the first promptings of guilt; the restraining influence it exercises over the beginning of the thought which, if indulged, would become a temptation; the check which it exerts over the gradual declension towards the state—never suddenly attained—in which crime no longer revolts, and punishment no longer terrifies.

## Unknown Number of Lives Saved

As for what is called the failure of death punishment, who is able to judge of that? We partly know who those are whom it has not deterred; but who is there who knows whom it has deterred, or how many human beings it has saved who would have lived to be murderers if that awful association had not been thrown round the idea of murder from their earliest infancy? Let us not forget that the most imposing fact loses its power over the imagination if it is made too cheap. When a punishment fit only for the most atrocious crimes is lavished on small offences until human feeling recoils from it, then, indeed, it ceases to intimidate, because it ceases to be believed in.

The failure of capital punishment in cases of theft is easily accounted for: the thief did not believe that it would be inflicted. He had learnt by experience that jurors would perjure themselves rather than find him guilty; that Judges would seize any excuse for not sentencing him to death, or for recommending him to mercy; and that if neither jurors nor Judges were merciful, there were still hopes from an authority above both. When things had come to this pass it was high time to give up the vain attempt. When it is impossible to inflict a punishment, or when its infliction becomes a public scandal, the idle threat cannot too soon disappear from the statute book. And in the case of the host of offences which were formerly capital, I heartily rejoice that it did become impracticable to execute the law.

---

## Deserved Retribution

Capital execution upon the deadly poisoner and the midnight assassin is not only necessary for the safety of society, it is the fit and deserved retribution of their crimes. By it alone is divine and human justice fulfilled.

Samuel Hand, *The North American Review*, December 1881.

---

If the same state of public feeling comes to exist in the case of murder; if the time comes when jurors refuse to find a murderer guilty; when Judges will not sentence him to death, or will recommend him to mercy; or when, if juries and Judges do not flinch from their duty, Home Secretaries, under pressure of deputations and memorials, shrink from theirs, and the threat becomes, as it became in the other cases, a mere *brutum fulmen*; then, indeed, it may become necessary to do in this case what has been done in those—to abrogate the penalty. That time may come—my hon. Friend thinks that it has nearly come. I hardly know whether he lamented it or boasted of it; but he and his Friends are entitled to the boast: for if it comes it will be their doing, and they will have gained what I cannot but call a fatal victory, for they will have achieved it by bringing about, if they will forgive me for saying so, an enervation, an effeminacy, in the general mind of the country. For what else than effeminacy is it to be so much more shocked by taking a man's life than by depriving him of all that makes life desirable or valuable? Is death, then, the greatest of all earthly ills? *Usque adeone mori miserum est?* [Is it, indeed, so dreadful a thing to die?] Has it not been from of old one chief part of a manly education to make us

31

despise death—teaching us to account it, if an evil at all, by no means high in the list of evils; at all events, as an inevitable one, and to hold, as it were, our lives in our hands, ready to be given or risked at any moment, for a sufficiently worthy object? I am sure that my hon. Friends know all this as well, and have as much of all these feelings as any of the rest of us; possibly more. But I cannot think that this is likely to be the effect of their teaching on the general mind.

## The Value of Human Life

I cannot think that the cultivating of a peculiar sensitiveness of conscience on this one point, over and above what result from the general cultivation of the moral sentiments, is permanently consistent with assigning in our own minds to the fact of death no more than the degree of relative importance which belongs to it among the other incidents of our humanity. The men of old cared too little about death, and gave their own lives or took those of others with equal recklessness. Our danger is of the opposite kind, lest we should be so much shocked by death, in general and in the abstract, as to care too much about it in individual cases, both those of other people and our own, which call for its being risked. And I am not putting things at the worst, for it is proved by the experience of other countries that horror of the executioner by no means necessarily implies horror of the assassin. The stronghold, as we all know, of hired assassination in the 18th century was Italy; yet it is said that in some of the Italian populations the infliction of death by sentence of law was in the highest degree offensive and revolting to popular feeling. Much has been said of the sanctity of human life, and the absurdity of supposing that we can teach respect for life by ourselves destroying it. But I am surprised at the employment of this argument, for it is one which might be brought against any punishment whatever. It is not human life only, not human life as such, that ought to be sacred to us, but human feelings. The human capacity of suffering is what we should cause to be respected, not the mere capacity of existing. And we may imagine somebody asking how we can teach people not to inflict suffering by ourselves inflicting it? But to this I should answer—all of us would answer—that to deter by suffering from inflicting suffering is not only possible, but the very purpose of penal justice. Does fining a criminal show want of respect for property, or imprisoning him, for personal freedom? Just as unreasonable is it to think that to take the life of a man who has taken that of another is to show want of regard for human life. We show, on the contrary, most emphatically our regard for it, by the adoption of a rule that he who violates that right in another forfeits it for himself, and that while no other crime that

32

he can commit deprives him of his right to live, this shall.

There is one argument against capital punishment, even in extreme cases, which I cannot deny to have weight. . . . It is this—that if by an error of justice an innocent person is put to death, the mistake can never be corrected; all compensation, all reparation for the wrong is impossible. This would be indeed a serious objection if these miserable mistakes—among the most tragical occurrences in the whole round of human affairs—could not be made extremely rare. The argument is invincible where the mode of criminal procedure is dangerous to the innocent, or where the Courts of Justice are not trusted. And this probably is the reason why the objection to an irreparable punishment began (as I believe it did) earlier, and is more intense and more widely diffused, in some parts of the Continent of Europe than it is here. There are on the continent great and enlightened countries, in which the criminal procedure is not so favourable to innocence, does not afford the same security against erroneous conviction, as it does among us; countries where the Courts of Justice seem to think they fail in their duty unless they find somebody guilty; and in their really laudable desire to hunt guilt from its hiding-places, expose themselves to a serious danger of condemning the innocent. If our own procedure and Courts of Justice afforded ground for similar apprehension, I should be the first to join in withdrawing the power of inflicting irreparable punishment from such tribunals. But we all know that the defects of our procedure are the very opposite.

---

### Perish the Murderers

It is better that the murderer should perish than that innocent men and women should have their throats cut. A witty Frenchman lately wrote a pamphlet on this subject, and said—

"I am all for abolishing the penalty of death, if Messieurs the Assassins would only set the example."

Mr. Gregory, from debate before England's Parliament, April 21, 1868.

---

Our rules of evidence are even too favourable to the prisoner: and juries and Judges carry out the maxim, "It is better that ten guilty should escape than that one innocent person should suffer," not only to the letter, but beyond the letter. Judges are most anxious to point out, and juries to allow for, the barest possibility of the prisoner's innocence. No human judgment is infallible: such sad cases as my hon. Friend cited will sometimes occur; but in so grave a case as that of murder, the accused, in our system, has always the benefit of the merest shadow of a doubt. And this suggests another consideration very germane to the question. The very fact that death punishment is more shocking than any other to the imagination, necessarily renders the courts of Justice more scrupulous in requiring the fullest evidence of guilt. Even that which is the greatest objection to capital punishment, the impossibility of correcting an error once committed, must make, and does make, juries and Judges more careful in forming their opinion, and more jealous in their scrutiny of the evidence.

If the substitution of penal servitude for death in cases of murder should cause any relaxation in this conscientious scrupulosity, there would be a great evil to set against the real, but I hope rare, advantage of being able to make reparation to a condemned person who was afterwards discovered to be innocent. In order that the possibility of correction may be kept open wherever the chance of this sad contingency is more than infinitesimal, it is quite right that the Judge should recommend to the Crown a commutation of the sentence, not solely when the proof of guilt is open to the smallest suspicion, but whenever there remains anything unexplained and mysterious in the case, raising a desire for more light, or making it likely that further information may at some future time be obtained.

## Against Total Abolition

I would also suggest that whenever the sentence is commuted the grounds of the commutation should, in some authentic form, be made known to the public. Thus much I willingly concede to my hon. Friend; but on the question of total abolition I am inclined to hope that the feeling of the country is not with him, and that the limitation of death punishment to the cases referred to in the Bill of last year will be generally considered sufficient. The mania which existed a short time ago for paring down all our punishments seems to have reached its limits, and not before it was time. We were in danger of being left without any effectual punishment, except for small offences. . . .

I think . . . that in the case of most offences, except those against property, there is more need of strengthening our punishments than of weakening them: and that severer sentences, with an apportionment of them to the different kinds of offences which shall approve itself better than at present to the moral sentiments of the community, are the kind of reform of which our penal system now stands in need.

*"Putting men to death in cold blood by human law . . . seems to me a most pernicious and brutalizing practice."*

# The Death Penalty Is State-Sanctioned Murder (1872)

Horace Greeley

Horace Greeley is a true American success story. Having grown up in abject poverty and with little education, Greeley founded the *New York Tribune* in 1841 and made it one of the most influential papers in the country. A social reformer, Greeley advocated temperance, women's rights, and a homestead law. In the following viewpoint Greeley addresses four points he believes prove the death penalty is dangerous and brutal.

As you read, consider the following questions:

1. Why does the author argue the death penalty is now obsolete?
2. Why does Greeley believe the death penalty sanctions revenge?

Horace Greeley, *Hints Toward Reforms in Lectures, Addresses, and Other Writings.* New York: Harper & Brothers, 1850.

Is it ever justifiable . . . to [kill] malefactors by sentence of law? I answer Yes, *provided* Society can in no other way be secured against a repetition of the culprit's offence. In committing a murder, for instance, he has proved himself capable of committing more murders—perhaps many. The possibility of a thousand murders is developed in his one act of felonious homicide. Call his moral state depravity, insanity, or whatever you please, he is manifestly a ferocious, dangerous animal, who can not safely be permitted to go at large. Society must be secured against the reasonable probability of his killing others, and, where that can only be effected by taking his life, his life must be taken.

—But suppose him to be in New-England, New-York or Pennsylvania—arrested, secured and convicted—Society's rebel, outcast and prisoner of war—taken with arms in his hands. Here are prison-cells wherefrom escape is impossible; and if there be any fear of his assaulting his keeper or others, that may be most effectively prevented. Is it expedient or salutary to crush the life out of this helpless, abject, pitiable wretch?

## A Sorrowful Mistake

I for one think it decidedly *is not*—that it is a sorrowful mistake and barbarity to do any such thing. In saying this, I do not assume to decide whether Hanging or Imprisonment for Life is the severer penalty. I should wish to understand clearly the moral state of the prisoner before I attempted to guess; and, even then, I know too little of the scenes of untried being which lie next beyond the confines of this mortal existence to say whether it were better for any penitent or hardened culprit to be hung next month or left in prison to die a natural death. What is best for that culprit I leave to God, who knows when is the fit time for him to die. My concern is with Society—the moral it teaches, the conduct it tacitly enjoins. And I feel that the choking to death of this culprit works harm, in these respects, namely:

1. *It teaches and sanctions Revenge.* There is a natural inclination in man to return injury for injury, evil for evil. It is the exciting cause of many murders as well as less flagrant crimes. It stands in no need of stimulation—its prompt repression at all times is one of the chief trials even of good men. But A.B. has committed a murder, is convicted of and finally hung for it. Bill, Dick and Jim, three apprentices of ordinary understanding and attainments, beg away or run away to witness the hanging. Ask either of them, 'What is this man hung for?' and the prompt, correct answer will be, 'Because he killed C.D.'—not 'To prevent his killing others,' nor yet 'To prevent others from killing.' Well: the three enjoy the spectacle and turn away satisfied. On their way

36

home, a scuffle is commenced in fun, but gradually changes to a fight, wherein one finds himself down with two holding and beating him. Though sorely exasperated and severely suffering, he can not throw them off, but he can reach with one hand the knife in his vest pocket. Do you fancy he will be more or less likely to use it because of that moral spectacle which Society has just proffered for his delectation and improvement? You may say Less if you can, but I say More! many times more! You may preach to him that Revenge is right for Society but wrong for him till your head is gray, and he perhaps may listen to you—but not till after he has opened his knife and made a lunge with it.

---

## Death Penalty Unnecessary

It is not necessary to hang the murderer in order to guard society against him, and to prevent him from repeating the crime. If it were, we should hang the maniac, who is the most dangerous murderer. Society may defend itself by other means than by destroying life. Massachusetts can build prisons strong enough to secure the community forever against convicted felons.

Robert Rantoul Jr., *Report to the Legislature*, 1836.

---

*2. It tends to weaken and destroy the natural horror of bloodshed.* Man has a natural horror of taking the life of his fellow man. His instincts revolt at it—his conscience condemns it—his frame shudders at the thought of it. But let him see first one and then another strung up between heaven and earth and choked to death, with due formalities of Law and solemnities of Religion— the slayer not accounted an evil-doer but an executor of the State's just decree, a pillar of the Social edifice—and his horror of bloodshed *per se* sensibly and rapidly oozes away, and he comes to look at killing men as quite the thing provided there be adequate reason for it. But what reason? and whose? The law slays the slayer; but in his sight the corrupter or calumniator of his wife or sister, the traducer of his character, the fraudulent bankrupt who has involved and ruined his friend, is every whit as great a villain as the man-slayer, and deserving of as severe a punishment. Yet the Law makes no provision for such punishment—hardly for any punishment at all—and what shall he do? He can not consent that the guilty go 'unwhipt of justice,' so he takes his rifle and deals out full measure of it. He is but doing as Society has taught him by example. War, dueling, bloody affrays, &c., find their nourishment and support in the Gallows.

3. *It facilitates and often insures the escape of the guilty from any punishment by human law.*—Jurors (whether for or against Capital

Punishment) dread to convict where the crime is Death. Human judgment is fallible; human testimony may mislead. Witnesses often lie—sometimes conspire to lie plausibly and effectively. Circumstances often strongly point to a conclusion which is after all a false one. The real murderers sometimes conspire to fasten suspicion on some innocent person, and so arrange the circumstances that he can hardly escape their toils. Sometimes they appear in court as witnesses against him, and swear the crime directly upon him. A single legal work contains a list of one hundred cases in which men were hung for crimes which they were afterward proved entirely innocent of. And for every such case there have doubtless been many wherein juries, unwilling to take life where there was a *possibility* of innocence, have given the prisoner the benefit of a very faint doubt and acquitted him. Had the penalty been Imprisonment, they would have convicted, notwithstanding the bare possibility of his innocence, since any future developments in his favor, through the retraction of witnesses, the clearing up of circumstances, or the confession of the actual culprit, would at once lead to his liberation and to an earnest effort by the community to repay him for his unmerited ignominy and suffering. But choke the prisoner to death, and any development in his favor is thenceforth too late. Next year may prove him innocent beyond cavil nor doubt; but of what avail is that to the victim over whose grave the young grass is growing? And thus, through the inexorable character of the Death-Penalty, hundreds of the innocent suffer an undeserved and ignominious death, while tens of thousands of the guilty escape any punishment by human law.

## Sympathizing with the Criminal

4. *It excites a pernicious sympathy for the convict.*—We ought ever to be merciful toward the sinful and guilty, remembering our own misdeeds and imperfections. We ought to regard with a benignant compassion those whom Crime has doomed to suffer. But the criminal is not a hero, nor a martyr, and should not be made to resemble one. A crowd of ten to fifty thousand persons, witnessing the infliction of the law's just penalty on an offender, and half of them sobbing and crying from sympathy for his fate, is not a wholesome spectacle—far otherwise. The impression it makes is not that of the majesty and Divine benignity of Law—the sovereignty and beneficence of Justice. Thousands are hoping, praying, entreating that a pardon may yet come—some will accuse the Executive of cruelty and hardness of heart in withholding it. While this furnace of sighs is at red heat, this tempest of sobs in full career, the culprit is swung off—a few faint; many shudder; more feel an acute shock of pain; while the great mass adjourn to take a general drink, some

of them swearing that *this* hanging was a great shame—that the man did not really deserve it. Do you fancy the greater number have imbibed and will profit by the intended lesson?

**Capital Punishment**

—But I do not care to pile argument on argument, consideration on consideration, in opposition to the expediency, in this day and section, of putting men to death in cold blood by human law. It seems to me a most pernicious and brutalizing practice. Indeed, the recent enactments of our own, with most if not all of the Free States, whereby Executions are henceforth to take place in private, or in the presence of a few select witnesses only, seem clearly to admit the fact. They certainly imply that Executions are of no use as examples—that they rather tend to make criminals than to reform those already depraved. When I see any business or vocation sneaking and skulking in dark lanes and little by-streets which elude observation, I conclude that those who follow such business feel at least doubtful of its utility and beneficence. They may *argue* that it is 'a necessary evil,' but they can hardly put faith in their own logic. When I see the bright array of many-colored liquor bottles, which formerly filled flauntingly the post of honor in every tip-top hotel, now hustled away into some sideroom, and finally down into a dark basement, out of the sight and knowledge of all but those who especially seek them, I say exultingly, 'Good for so much! one more 'hoist, and they will be—where they should be—out of sight 'and reach altogether:'—so, when I see the Gallows, once the denizen of some swelling eminence, the cynosure of ten thousand eyes, 'the observed of all observers,' skulking and hiding itself from public view in jail-yards, shutting itself up in prisons, I say, 'You have taken the right road! Go 'ahead! One more drive, and your detested, rickety frame 'is out of the sight of civilized man for ever!'

*"It is the finality of the death penalty which instils fear into the heart of every murderer, and it is this fear of punishment which protects society."*

# Capital Punishment Is a Safeguard for Society (1925)

Robert E. Crowe

In early 1925, when Judge Robert E. Crowe wrote his opinion of the death penalty, he was state's attorney for Cook County, Illinois. He had just been the prosecutor in the widely publicized trial of Nathan Leopold and Richard Loeb, two young men who were charged with the murder of a young boy. The first World War had not been over for long and America was beginning to focus again on its own growing problem of crime. In this viewpoint Crowe defends the American legal system and the necessity of ridding society of murderers in order to secure safety for its members and deter further murders.

As you read, consider the following questions:

1. Why does the author believe that a murderer is a danger to all of society?
2. How does Crowe think the American system protects the accused criminal?
3. What arguments does the author offer for his statement that capital punishment is a deterrent to crime?

Robert E. Crowe, "Capital Punishment Protects Society," *The Forum*, February 1925.

I believe that the penalty for murder should be death. I urge capital punishment for murder not because I believe that society wishes to take the life of a murderer but because society does not wish to lose its own. I advocate this extreme and irrevocable penalty because the punishment is commensurate with the crime. The records, I believe, will show that the certainty of punishment is a deterrent of crime. As the law is written in most of the States of the Union, every other form of punishment is revocable at the will of an individual.

It is the finality of the death penalty which instils fear into the heart of every murderer, and it is this fear of punishment which protects society. Murderers are not punished for revenge. The man with the life blood of another upon his hands is a menace to the life of every citizen. He should be removed from society for the sake of society. In his removal, society is sufficiently protected, but only provided it is a permanent removal. I should like to see the experiment of the inexorable infliction of the death penalty upon all deliberate murderers tried out in every State of the Union for a sufficient period of time to demonstrate whether or not it is the most effective and most certain means of checking the appalling slaughter of innocent, peaceful, and law-abiding citizens which has gone on without check for so many years, and which is increasing at a rate which has won for the United States of America the disgrace of being known as "the most lawless nation claiming place among the civilized nations of the world."

### Duty to Society

The attitude which society must take toward offenders—great as well as small—must not be confused with the attitude which the individual quite properly may assume. Neither may officers of the law nor leaders of public thought, if they are mindful of the duty which they owe to society, advocate a substitution of any other penalty for murder than that penalty which will give to society the greatest degree of protection. . . .

In cases where—in a properly constituted court over whose deliberations a properly elected or appointed judge has presided and in which, after hours and days and sometimes weeks of patient and deliberate inquiry, a jury of twelve men selected in the manner which the law provides—a man charged with murder has been found guilty and sentenced to death, it is an unpardonable abuse of the great power of executive clemency to nullify the verdict by commuting the sentence to life imprisonment. It is in effect a usurpation by the executive authority of the state of powers and duties deliberately and expressly assigned by the representatives of the people in the constitution to the judicial branch alone.

I do not believe that the American Bar is ready to plead guilty to the charge which this action infers that lawyers for the prosecution and lawyers for the defense are so venal, corrupt, and bloodthirsty through ulterior motives as to deliberately conspire with an unrighteous judge, an unprincipled or irresponsible jury and witnesses prompted solely by the spirit of revenge to doom to death any man on a charge of murder unless the testimony truly shows him guilty beyond all reasonable doubt. . . .

## Faith in Americans

It is because of my faith and trust in the integrity of our American citizens that I believe that there is no considerable danger that the innocent man will be convicted and that society may be charged that in a blind zeal to protect itself against murder it actually commits murder by the infliction of the death penalty.

The man who kills is society's greatest enemy. He has set up his own law. He is an anarchist—the foe of all civilized government. If anarchy is not to be met with anarchy, it must be met by the laws, and these laws must be enforced. . . .

---

### Penalize Offenders

If we want order, we must stop being soft-headed sentimentalists when it comes to penalizing offenders. The murder rate in the United States rises to a scandalous figure. Of the many who kill, comparatively few are ever arrested, still fewer convicted, fewer yet ever see the inside of a felon's cell; only rarely is the murderer punished as the law says he shall be. A life term is commonly a short vacation at State expense with nothing to do but eat the fruit of others' industry. Americans are not a nation of murder lovers. We merely seem to be. We are made to seem to be by ill-prepared judges, woozy jurors, and a public opinion sentimentally inclined to sympathize more with the perpetrators than the victims of major crimes. This country needs a rededication to the everlasting truth that the fear of prompt and adequate punishment is the best deterrent for gentlemen tempted to slay. This violates long book-shelves of theory.

*Cleveland Plain Dealer*, January 25, 1925.

---

Why are there so few violations of the laws of the United States? When a man files his income tax schedule, why does he hire an auditor to see that he makes no mistake, and why does the same man when he goes before our Boards of Assessors and Boards of Review and schedules his personal property for taxation in Chicago as well as elsewhere conceal millions upon which he should be taxed? Why? Because when you get into the United States court after having violated the laws of the United

States, if you are guilty, no plea of mercy, however eloquent or by whomsoever delivered, will cheat the law there.

We hear much about England. There murder is murder. Justice is swift and sure. There are fewer murders in the entire Kingdom of Great Britain yearly than there are in the city of Chicago.

In recent years the American public has been influenced to some extent by an active, persistent, and systematic agitation based upon an unfortunate and misplaced sympathy for persons accused of crime. I say unfortunate and misplaced sympathy because it is a sympathy guided by emotion and impulse rather than upon reason and compassion for the prisoners at the bar. It is so deep and soul stirring that it loses its sense of proportion. It forgets the life that was blotted out. It forgets the broken-hearted left behind. It forgets the fatherless and sometimes homeless children which should be the real object of pity. It forgets that they become charges upon the state and it also forgets that there has been established a broken home—the one in the group of homes from which twice as many criminals come as from those which remain intact.

Opponents of capital punishment think somewhat along the same lines. They forget that murder is inexorable and that the victim never returns. They forget that society is protected best by punishment which is proportionate to the crime. They are moved to abolish hanging because it is an unwholesome spectacle. They overlook the unwholesome and harrowing aspects of a murder scene.

Some who admit the justice of capital punishment deny its necessity. They argue that in taking the life of an offender society is wreaking vengeance upon a helpless individual, while, as a matter of fact, the exact opposite is true. If an individual were to slay another who was guilty of murder, especially if he had no fear of him, the act would be prompted by revenge. And when we realize that many of our present-day murderers are professional criminals whose victims were slain in the course of holdups, robberies, and other crimes committed for profit, and that the victim was killed deliberately on the theory that dead men can make no identifications, we know at once that they did not kill for revenge and that they had no malice against the individual they killed. Society for its own protection should make it impossible for these men to kill again.

### Crime Against Society

Murder like all other crime is a crime against society. It is for assault upon society that the state inflicts punishment. Too many confuse the relation of the victim of a crime with that of the interest of the state in the prosecution of criminals. The state is impersonal. It is the voice for all of the people expressed

44

by a voting majority. What happens or has happened to any individual is not of great importance. The civil courts exist for the adjudication of the individual and personal wrong. The criminal court exists to punish those who have offended against the state. He who violates the criminal code offends against and injures us all. When he injures to the extent of unlawfully taking human life, he has committed a grave and irreparable injury.

Punishment of the slayer will not bring back life to the victim. But punishment for crime is not inflicted upon any theory of relationship to the victim except to consider the fact that the victim was a part of society and that in wronging the individual that society itself has been assaulted.

## Responsibility for Actions

I am not ready to agree to the theory that all or most murderers are not responsible for their acts. I believe that man is entitled to free will and that except in rare instances he is both morally and legally responsible for all his acts. I cannot accept the theory that murderers should not be punished for their crime because they are irresponsible. If they are so irresponsible as to constitute a danger to society, I do not believe that society can carefully preserve in existence the danger they represent. I believe that society is justified in destroying even the irresponsible murderer if he is known to imperil the life of other persons. There should be no sentiment about it. Persons whose existence means death and disaster to others who have done no wrong have no claim upon society for anything—not even for life itself.

## Safety of Citizens

Nothing is more remarkable in the evolution of a community than the growing regard for human life. A community is held to be civilized, or not, in exact proportion to the safety of the common citizen. When the life of an individual is unjustly taken by another individual, the horror of the community for such an act cannot be adequately and proportionately manifested except as the community surmounts sentiment and exacts the life of the killer in payment—after a trial, where all opportunity of defense is accorded, and after all possible human excuses and palliations have been alleged, tested, and found insufficient.

R.L. Calder, "Is Capital Punishment Right? A Debate," *The Forum*, September 1928.

Few men who murder have previously lived blameless lives. The act of murder is the climax—a cumulative effect of countless previous thoughts and acts. The man's conduct depends upon his philosophy of life. Those who want to grow up to be respectable and useful citizens in the community have a correct philosophy. Those who want to excel in crime, those who tear down instead of building up, deliberately choose to adopt the wrong philosophy of life and to make their conduct correspond with it.

Society and particularly the state would not be much concerned with individual codes of conduct if, at the present time, they were not adopted by the youths of the land and were not creating an army of virtual anarchists who look upon the criminal code, including that part of it forbidding murder, as a mere convention of society which "advanced thinking" and crazy social theories permit them to set aside as a matter of no consequence.

Because some of the youth of our population are saturated with these ideas, we are asked to accept fantastic notions, abnormal actions, and even defiance, disregard, and violation of the law, as the reason for turning them loose when charged with murder. We are compelled to listen to the weirdest, wildest, and most fantastic theories expounded by expert witnesses to show why capital punishment should not be inflicted. . . .

If the United States of America has the power to take boys of eighteen years of age and send them to their death in the front line trenches in countries overseas in defense of our laws, I believe that the state has an equal right to take the lives of murderers of like age for violating the mandate of God and man, "Thou shalt not kill."

### Deterrent of Crime

I base my belief that capital punishment is a deterrent of crime upon the fact that where capital punishment has been inflicted for even a comparatively small period and in a relatively small number of cases, there subsequently has been an immediate decrease in murder. Those who argue against capital punishment should bear in mind that where capital punishment has actually been inflicted, this has been the result. But, capital punishment has never been given a fair trial throughout this country over a sufficient period of time and in a sufficient number of cases to justify the assumption that it is not a deterrent of murder.

Until American society finds a way to protect itself from the murder of its members, this country will continue to be known as "the most lawless nation claiming place among the civilized nations of the world." I am not proud of that appellation. I hang my head in shame whenever I hear it. I believe society should have no hesitancy in springing the trap every time the noose can be put around a murderer's neck.

> *"It is hardly probable that the great majority of people refrain from killing their neighbors because they are afraid; they refrain because they never had the inclination."*

# Capital Punishment Will Not Safeguard Society (1928)

Clarence Darrow

Clarence Darrow was a Chicago lawyer who became famous for his handling of criminal and labor cases. He chose to defend those whom he considered social unfortunates. He argued on behalf of more than one hundred people charged with murder, none of whom were sentenced to death. Although he retired in 1927, he continued to write prolifically on the causes of crime and to argue vehemently for the abolition of the death penalty. His most famous courtroom pleas are included in the book *Attorney for the Damned*. In the following viewpoint, Darrow maintains that capital punishment is no deterrent to crime. He advances his theory that as victims of their culture, criminals need to be treated more humanely.

As you read, consider the following questions:

1. To what does Darrow attribute the causes of crime, specifically murder?
2. What arguments does the author offer to support his belief that capital punishment is no deterrent to murder?

Clarence Darrow, "The Futility of the Death Penalty," *The Forum*, September 1928.

Little more than a century ago, in England, there were over two hundred offenses that were punishable with death. The death sentence was passed upon children under ten years old. And every time the sentimentalist sought to lessen the number of crimes punishable by death, the self-righteous said no, that it would be the destruction of the state; that it would be better to kill for more transgressions rather than for less.

Today, both in England and America, the number of capital offenses has been reduced to a very few, and capital punishment would doubtless be abolished altogether were it not for the self-righteous, who still defend it with the same old arguments. Their major claim is that capital punishment decreases the number of murders, and hence, that the state must retain the institution as its last defense against the criminal.

It is my purpose in this article to prove, first, that capital punishment is no deterrent to crime; and second, that the state continues to kill its victims, not so much to defend society against them—for it could do that equally well by imprisonment—but to appease the mob's emotions of hatred and revenge.

### The Criminal Disease

Behind the idea of capital punishment lies false training and crude views of human conduct. People do evil things, say the judges, lawyers, and preachers, because of depraved hearts. Human conduct is not determined by the causes which determine the conduct of other animal and plant life in the universe. For some mysterious reason human beings act as they please; and if they do not please to act in a certain way, it is because, having the power of choice, they deliberately choose to act wrongly. The world once applied this doctrine to disease and insanity in men. It was also applied to animals, and even inanimate things were once tried and condemned to destruction. The world knows better now, but the rule has not yet been extended to human beings.

The simple fact is that every person starts life with a certain physical structure, more or less sensitive, stronger or weaker. He is played upon by everything that reaches him from without, and in this he is like everything else in the universe, inorganic matter as well as organic. How a man will act depends upon the character of his human machine, and the strength of the various stimuli that affect it. Everyone knows that this is so in disease and insanity. Most investigators know that it applies to crime. But the great mass of people still sit in judgment, robed with self-righteousness, and determine the fate of their less fortunate fellows. When this question is studied like any other, we shall then know how to get rid of most of the conduct that we call "criminal," just as we are now getting rid of much of the disease that once afflicted mankind.

If crime were really the result of willful depravity, we should be ready to concede that capital punishment may serve as a deterrent to the criminally inclined. But it is hardly probable that the great majority of people refrain from killing their neighbors because they are afraid; they refrain because they never had the inclination. Human beings are creatures of habit and, as a rule, they are not in the habit of killing. The circumstances that lead to killings are manifold, but in a particular individual the inducing cause is not easily found. In one case, homicide may have been induced by indigestion in the killer; in another, it may be traceable to some weakness inherited from a remote ancestor; but that it results from *something* tangible and understandable, if all the facts were known, must be plain to everyone who believes in cause and effect.

## Punishment No Cure for Crime

There is no deterrent in the menace of the gallows.

Cruelty and viciousness are not abolished by cruelty and viciousness—not even by legalized cruelty and viciousness. . . .

Our penal system has broken down because it is built upon the sand—founded on the basis of force and violence—instead of on the basis of Christian care of our fellow men, of moral and mental human development, of the conscientious performance by the State of its duty to the citizen.

We cannot cure murder by murder.

We must adopt another and better system.

William Randolph Hearst, *The Congressional Digest*, August/September 1927.

Of course, no one will be converted to this point of view by statistics of crime. In the first place, it is impossible to obtain reliable ones; and in the second place, the conditions to which they apply are never the same. But if one cares to analyze the figures, such as we have, it is easy to trace the more frequent causes of homicide. The greatest number of killings occur during attempted burglaries and robberies. The robber knows that penalties for burglary do not average more than five years in prison. He also knows that the penalty for murder is death or life imprisonment. Faced with this alternative, what does the burglar do when he is detected and threatened with arrest? He shoots to kill. He deliberately takes the chance of death to save himself from a five-year term in prison. It is therefore as obvious as anything can be that fear of death has no effect in diminishing homicides of this kind, which are more numerous than any other type.

The next largest number of homicides may be classed as "sex murders." Quarrels between husbands and wives, disappointed love, or love too much requited cause many killings. They are the result of primal emotions so deep that the fear of death has not the slightest effect in preventing them. Spontaneous feelings overflow in criminal acts, and consequences do not count. Then there are cases of sudden anger, uncontrollable rage. The fear of death never enters into such cases; if the anger is strong enough, consequences are not considered until too late. The old-fashioned stories of men deliberately plotting and committing murder in cold blood have little foundation in real life. Such killings are so rare that they need not concern us here. The point to be emphasized is that practically all homicides are manifestations of well-recognized human emotions, and it is perfectly plain that the fear of excessive punishment does not enter into them.

In addition to these personal forces which overwhelm weak men and lead them to commit murder, there are also many social and economic forces which must be listed among the causes of homicides, and human beings have even less control over these than over their own emotions. It is often said that in America there are more homicides in proportion to population than in England. This is true. There are likewise more in the United States than in Canada. But such comparisons are meaningless until one takes into consideration the social and economic differences in the countries compared. Then it becomes apparent why the homicide rate in the United States is higher. Canada's population is largely rural; that of the United States is crowded into cities whose slums are the natural breeding places of crime. Moreover, the population of England and Canada is homogeneous, while the United States has gathered together people of every color from every nation in the world. Racial differences intensify social, religious, and industrial problems, and the confusion which attends this indiscriminate mixing of races and nationalities is one of the most fertile sources of crime.

### Primitive Beliefs

Will capital punishment remedy these conditions? Of course it won't; but its advocates argue that the fear of this extreme penalty will hold the victims of adverse conditions in check. To this piece of sophistry the continuance and increase of crime in our large cities is a sufficient answer. No, the plea that capital punishment acts as a deterrent to crime will not stand. The real reason why this barbarous practice persists in a so-called civilized world is that people still hold the primitive belief that the taking of one human life can be atoned for by taking another. It is the age-old obsession with punishment that keeps the official headsman busy plying his trade.

And it is precisely upon this point that I would build my case against capital punishment. Even if one grants that the idea of punishment is sound, crime calls for something more—for careful study, for an understanding of causes, for proper remedies. To attempt to abolish crime by killing the criminal is the easy and foolish way out of a serious situation. Unless a remedy deals with the conditions which foster crime, criminals will breed faster than the hangman can spring his trap. Capital punishment ignores the causes of crime just as completely as the primitive witch doctor ignored the causes of disease; and, like the methods of the witch doctor, it is not only ineffective as a remedy, but is positively vicious in at least two ways. In the first place, the spectacle of state executions feeds the basest passions of the mob. And in the second place, so long as the state rests content to deal with crime in this barbaric and futile manner, society will be lulled by a false sense of security, and effective methods of dealing with crime will be discouraged. . . .

## Crime in England

For the last five or six years, in England and Wales, the homicides reported by the police range from sixty-five to seventy a year. Death sentences meted out by jurors have averaged about thirty-five, and hangings, fifteen. More than half of those convicted by juries were saved by appeals to the Home Office. But in America there is no such percentage of lives saved after conviction. Governors are afraid to grant clemency. If they did, the newspapers and the populace would refuse to reelect them.

---

### Failure to Instill Fear

It is a fact that a large percentage of murders are committed in the heat of passion, when the murderer is not in a position to reason; fear of the law plays no part at all. In the remaining few, whatever fear there may be is more than balanced by the belief on the part of the criminal that he is not going to get caught. There are also some who deliberately kill; but the knowledge that they will be caught and punished does not deter them.

Thomas Mott Osborne, "Thou Shalt Not Kill," *The Forum*, February 1925.

---

It is true that trials are somewhat prompter in England than America, but there no newspaper dares publish the details of any case until after the trial. In America the accused is often convicted by the public within twenty-four hours of the time a homicide occurs. The courts sidetrack all other business so that a homicide that is widely discussed may receive prompt attention. The road to the gallows is not only opened but greased for the opportunity of killing another victim. . . .

Human conduct is by no means so simple as our moralists have led us to believe. There is no sharp line separating good actions from bad. The greed for money, the display of wealth, the despair of those who witness the display, the poverty, oppression, and hopelessness of the unfortunate—all these are factors which enter into human conduct and of which the world takes no account. Many people have learned no other profession but robbery and burglary. The processions moving steadily through our prisons to the gallows are in the main made up of these unfortunates. And how do we dare to consider ourselves civilized creatures when, ignoring the causes of crime, we rest content to mete out harsh punishments to the victims of conditions over which they have no control?

Even now, are not all imaginative and humane people shocked at the spectacle of a killing by the state? How many men and women would be willing to act as executioners? How many fathers and mothers would want their children to witness an official killing? What kind of people read the sensational reports of an execution? If all right-thinking men and women were not ashamed of it, why would it be needful that judges and lawyers and preachers apologize for the barbarity? How can the state censure the cruelty of the man who—moved by strong passions, or acting to save his freedom, or influenced by weakness or fear—takes human life, when everyone knows that the state itself, after long premeditation and settled hatred, not only kills, but first tortures and bedevils its victims for weeks with the impending doom?

## More Humane Criminal Code

For the last hundred years the world has shown a gradual tendency to mitigate punishment. We are slowly learning that this way of controlling human beings is both cruel and ineffective. In England the criminal code has consistently grown more humane, until now the offenses punishable by death are reduced to practically one. If there is any reason for singling out this one, neither facts nor philosophy can possibly demonstrate it. There is no doubt whatever that the world is growing more humane and more sensitive and more understanding. The time will come when all people will view with horror the light way in which society and its courts of law now take human life; and when that time comes, the way will be clear to devise some better method of dealing with poverty and ignorance and their frequent by-products which we call crime.

CHAPTER

2

# Is the Death Penalty Just?

# Chapter Preface

The bomb that destroyed Oklahoma City's Alfred P. Murrah Federal Building on April 19, 1995, took the lives of 169 people. When two suspects were arrested in the case, U.S. attorney general Janet Reno announced that the government would seek the death penalty for the crime. Many people firmly believe that death sentences would be the appropriate punishments for those who caused so many deaths. But a few argue that executing the bombers would only compound the violence.

Among those who oppose the death penalty in all cases are the editors of the Catholic weekly *Commonweal*. Although they believe that the "mass murder" in Oklahoma City is a crime "as senseless as it is evil, as cruel as it is stupid," they nevertheless insist that the perpetrators should not receive death sentences. They maintain that executing murderers—even the killers of 169 people—sends a contradictory message about the sanctity of human life. "By killing people for killing people we become like the killers," they contend. Murder and capital punishment are equivalent, the editors assert, because both acts result in the taking of a human life. The death penalty is wrong, they argue, because it "is not a rejection of violence but a societal endorsement of violence."

But Paul Baumann, an associate editor of *Commonweal*, joins the majority of Americans in calling for death sentences for the Oklahoma City bombers. Disagreeing with his colleagues, he rejects their argument that the use of violence by society is unjust. He contends that the death penalty is the only punishment that can properly express Americans' moral outrage at this crime and maintain a sense of justice. "In imposing the death penalty for especially heinous crimes," Baumann asserts, "the law proclaims in unambiguous terms the value society places on innocent life and the absolute revulsion in which we hold such murders."

Though the Oklahoma City bombing was certainly among the deadliest crimes of the century, people disagree whether the death penalty is a fitting punishment. The viewpoints in the following chapter debate the moral and constitutional justness of capital punishment.

*"Allowing our government to kill citizens compromises the deepest moral values upon which this country was conceived: the inviolable dignity of human persons."*

# The Death Penalty Is Morally Unjust

Helen Prejean

Although the Bible clearly prescribes capital punishment in certain cases, modern-day Christians are divided on whether it is acceptable. In the following viewpoint, Helen Prejean explains that the death penalty was permitted in biblical times because its use was necessary to maintain social order. She contends, however, that Jesus' example of nonviolence precludes use of the death penalty and that in American society in the present capital punishment is too morally costly to be allowed. Prejean is a Catholic nun in the order of the Sisters of St. Joseph of Medaille. She is an anti–death penalty activist and the author of *Dead Man Walking*, from which this viewpoint is excerpted.

As you read, consider the following questions:

1. According to Prejean, what is the real intent of the "eye for eye" passage in the Bible?
2. What does the author say she personally believes is Jesus' ethical thrust?
3. What, according to the author, will it take to abolish the death penalty?

$I$ think of the running debate I engage in with "church" people about the death penalty. "Proof texts" from the Bible usually punctuate these discussions without regard for the cultural context or literary genre of the passages invoked. (Will D. Campbell, a Southern Baptist minister and writer, calls this use of scriptural quotations "biblical quarterbacking.")

It is abundantly clear that the Bible depicts murder as a crime for which death is considered the appropriate punishment, and one is hard-pressed to find a biblical "proof text" in either the Hebrew Testament or the New Testament which unequivocally refutes this. Even Jesus' admonition "Let him without sin cast the first stone," when he was asked the appropriate punishment for an adulteress (John 8:7)—the Mosaic law prescribed death—should be read in its proper context. This passage is an "entrapment" story, which sought to show Jesus' wisdom in besting his adversaries. It is not an ethical pronouncement about capital punishment.

## The Death Penalty in a Biblical Context

Similarly, the "eye for eye" passage from Exodus, which pro-death penalty advocates are fond of quoting, is rarely cited in its original context, in which it is clearly meant to limit revenge.

The passage, including verse 22, which sets the context reads:

> If, when men come to blows, they hurt a woman who is pregnant and she suffers a miscarriage, though she does not die of it, the man responsible must pay the compensation demanded of him by the woman's master; he shall hand it over after arbitration. But should she die, you shall give life for life, eye for eye, tooth for tooth, hand for hand, foot for foot, burn for burn, wound for wound, stroke for stroke. (Exodus 21: 22–25)

In the example given (patently patriarchal: the woman is considered the negotiable property of her male master), it is clear that punishment is to be measured out according to the seriousness of the offense. If the child is lost but not the mother, the punishment is less grave than if both mother and child are lost. *Only* an eye for an eye, *only* a life for a life is the intent of the passage. Restraint was badly needed. It was not uncommon for an offended family or clan to slaughter entire communities in retaliation for an offense against one of their members.

Even granting the call for restraint in this passage, it is nonetheless clear—here and in numerous other instances throughout the Hebrew Bible—that the punishment for murder was death.

But we must remember that such prescriptions of the Mosaic Law were promulgated in a seminomadic culture in which the preservation of a fragile society—without benefit of prisons and other institutions—demanded quick, effective, harsh punishment of offenders. And we should note the numerous other crimes for which the Bible prescribes death as punishment:

contempt of parents (Exodus 21:15, 17; Leviticus 24:17);

trespass upon sacred ground (Exodus 19:12–13; Numbers 1:51; 18:7);

sorcery (Exodus 22:18; Leviticus 20:27);

bestiality (Exodus 22:19; Leviticus 20: 15–16);

sacrifice to foreign gods (Exodus 22:20; Deuteronomy 13:1–9);

profaning the sabbath (Exodus 31:14);

adultery (Leviticus 20:10; Deuteronomy 22: 22–24);

incest (Leviticus 20:11–13);

homosexuality (Leviticus 20:13);

and prostitution (Leviticus 21:19; Deuteronomy 22: 13–21).

And this is by no means a complete list.

But no person with common sense would dream of appropriating such a moral code today, and it is curious that those who so readily invoke the "eye for an eye, life for life" passage are quick to shun other biblical prescriptions which also call for death, arguing that modern societies have evolved over the three thousand or so years since biblical times and no longer consider such exaggerated and archaic punishments appropriate.

## Capital Punishment Fosters a Climate of Violence

The North Dakota Catholic Conference opposes carrying out the death penalty as a means of dealing with crime in North Dakota. The fundamental purpose of all punishment is to preserve and enhance the common good. We must never lose sight of this purpose by disregarding the effects of resorting to violent death as a means of dealing with crime. A society that chooses violent death as a solution to a social problem gives official sanction to a climate of violence.

Each of us, as members of the community, participates in the punishment of offenders. We must not, therefore, approach such a matter lightly or leave it to the winds of public opinion. It demands great scrutiny and a rightly formed conscience. Above all, we must root our approach to punishment, especially punishment by death, in the respect for sanctity of human life and the dignity of all persons, and the preservation and enhancement of the common good.

North Dakota Catholic Conference, *Origins*, March 9, 1995.

Such nuances are lost, of course, in "biblical quarterbacking," and more and more I find myself steering away from such futile discussions. Instead, I try to articulate what I personally believe about Jesus and the ethical thrust he gave to humankind: an impetus toward compassion, a preference for disarming enemies without humiliating and destroying them, and a solidarity with poor and suffering people.

## A Diversion from Jesus' Teachings

So, what happened to the impetus of love and compassion Jesus set blazing into history?

The first Christians adhered closely to the way of life Jesus had taught. They died in amphitheaters rather than offer homage to worldly emperors. They refused to fight in emperors' wars. But then a tragic diversion happened, which Elaine Pagels has deftly explored in her book *Adam, Eve, and the Serpent:* in 313 C.E. (Common Era) the Emperor Constantine entered the Christian church.

Pagels says, "Christian bishops, once targets for arrest, torture, and execution, now received tax exemptions, gifts from the imperial treasury, prestige, and even influence at court; the churches gained new wealth, power and prominence."

Unfortunately, the exercise of power practiced by Christians in alliance with the Roman Empire—with its unabashed allegiance to the sword—soon bore no resemblance to the purely moral persuasion that Jesus had taught.

In the fifth century, Pagels points out, Augustine provided the theological rationale the church needed to justify the use of violence by church and state governments. Augustine persuaded church authorities that "original sin" so damaged every person's ability to make moral choices that external control by church and state authorities over people's lives was necessary and justified. The "wicked" might be "coerced by the sword" to "protect the innocent," Augustine taught. And thus was legitimated for Christians the authority of secular government to "control" its subjects by coercive and violent means—even punishment by death.

In the latter part of the twentieth century, however, two flares of hope—Mohandas K. Gandhi and Martin Luther King—have demonstrated that Jesus' counsel to practice compassion and tolerance even toward one's enemies can effect social change. Susan Jacoby, analyzing the moral power that Gandhi and King unleashed in their campaigns for social justice, finds a unique form of aggression:

"'If everyone took an eye for an eye,' Gandhi said, 'the whole world would be blind.' But Gandhi did not want to take anyone's eye; he wanted to force the British out of India. . . ."

*Nonviolence and nonaggression are generally regarded as interchangeable concepts—King and Gandhi frequently used them that way—but nonviolence, as employed by Gandhi in India and by King in the American South, might reasonably be viewed as a highly disciplined form of aggression. If one defines aggression in the primary dictionary sense of "attack," nonviolent resistance proved to be the most powerful attack imaginable on the powers King and Gandhi were trying to overturn. The writings of both men*

*are filled with references to love as a powerful force against oppres-*
*sion, and while the two leaders were not using the term "force" in*
*the military sense, they certainly regarded nonviolence as a tactical*
*weapon as well as an expression of high moral principle. The root*
*meaning of Gandhi's concept of* satyagraha . . . *is "holding on to*
*truth" . . . Gandhi also called* satyagraha *the "love force" or "soul*
*force" and explained that he had discovered "in the earliest stages*
*that pursuit of truth did not permit violence being inflicted on one's*
*opponent, but that he must be weaned from error by patience and*
*sympathy. . . . And patience means self-suffering." So the doctrine*
*came to mean vindication of truth, not by the infliction of suffering*
*on the opponent, but on one's self.*

*King was even more explicit on this point: the purpose of civil dis-*
*obedience, he explained many times, was to force the defenders of*
*segregation to commit brutal acts in public and thus arouse the*
*conscience of the world on behalf of those wronged by racism. King*
*and Gandhi did not succeed because they changed the hearts and*
*minds of southern sheriffs and British colonial administrators [al-*
*though they did, in fact, change some minds] but because they*
made the price of maintaining control too high for their opponents [emphasis mine].

That, I believe, is what it's going to take to abolish the death
penalty in this country: we must persuade the American people
that government killings are too costly for us, not only finan-
cially, but—more important—morally.

## The Moral Costs of the Death Penalty

The death penalty *costs* too much. Allowing our government to
kill citizens compromises the deepest moral values upon which
this country was conceived: the inviolable dignity of human
persons.

I have no doubt that we will one day abolish the death penalty
in America. It will come sooner if people like me who know the
truth about executions do our work well and educate the public.
It will come slowly if we do not. Because, finally, I know that it
is not a question of malice or ill will or meanness of spirit that
prompts our citizens to support executions. It is, quite simply,
that people don't know the truth of what is going on. That is not
by accident. The secrecy surrounding executions makes it possible for executions to continue. I am convinced that if executions
were made public, the torture and violence would be unmasked,
and we would be shamed into abolishing executions. We would
be embarrassed at the brutalization of the crowds that would
gather to watch a man or woman be killed. And we would be
humiliated to know that visitors from other countries—Japan,
Russia, Latin America, Europe—were watching us kill our own
citizens—we, who take pride in being the flagship of democracy
in the world.

*"A moral obligation requires civil government to punish crime, and consequently, to enforce capital punishment."*

# The Death Penalty Is Morally Just

Charles W. Colson

Some Christians believe that use of the death penalty is morally unacceptable. In the following viewpoint, Charles W. Colson argues that Christian ethics clearly support the power of society to enforce order and sustain justice. He contends that in order to maintain society's sense of justice, it is necessary to punish perpetrators of the worst crimes with the death penalty. Colson, who was imprisoned for his role in the Watergate scandal of the 1972 election, is the founder of Prison Fellowship Ministries in Washington, D.C. He is the author of several books on his prison and religious experiences.

As you read, consider the following questions:

1. What is the definition of justice given by Colson? What is his definition of mercy?
2. What is the "fundamental truth of biblical anthropology," according to the author?
3. According to Colson, what values is society dealing with in the debate over the death penalty?

Abridged from "Capital Punishment: A Personal Statement" by Charles Colson, working paper, Prison Fellowship, Washington, D.C., May 1995. Reprinted by permission of the author.

For as long as I can remember, I have opposed capital punishment. As a lawyer I observed how flawed the legal system is, and I concluded, as Judge Learned Hand once remarked, that it was better that a hundred guilty men go free than one innocent man be executed. I was also influenced by very libertarian views of government; I distrusted government too much to give power to take a human life to the judicial system.

Then as I became a Christian, I was confronted with the reality of Jesus' payment of the debt of human sin. I discovered that the operation of God's marvelous grace in our lives has profound implications for the way we live. Naturally, as I came to deal increasingly with ethical issues, I found myself seriously questioning whether the death penalty was an effective deterrent. My views were very much influenced by Deuteronomy 17 and the need for two eyewitnesses [to a crime]. I questioned whether the circumstantial evidence on which most are sentenced today in fact measures up to this standard of proof.

I still have grave reservations about the way in which capital punishment is administered in the United States, and I still do question whether it is a deterrent. (In fact, I remain convinced it is not a general deterrent.) But I must say that my views have changed and that I now favor capital punishment, at least in principle, but only in extreme cases when no other punishment can satisfy the demands of justice.

## Proportionate Justice

The reason for this is quite simple. Justice in God's eyes requires that the response to an offense—whether against God or against humanity—be proportionate. The *lex talionis*, the "law of the talion" [retaliation], served as a restraint, a limitation, that punishment would be no greater than the crime. Yet, implied therein is a standard that the punishment should be *at least as great* as the crime. One frequently finds among Christians the belief that Jesus' so-called "love ethic" sets aside the "law of the talion." To the contrary, Jesus affirms the divine basis of Old Testament ethics. Nowhere does Jesus set aside the requirements of civil law. Furthermore, it leads to a perversion of legal justice to confuse the sphere of private relations with that of civil law. While the thief on the cross found pardon in the sight of God ("Today you will be with me in Paradise"), that pardon did not extend to eliminating the consequences of his crime ("We are being justly punished, for we are receiving what we deserve for our deeds").

What about mercy? someone is inclined to ask. My response is simple. There can be no mercy where justice is not satisfied. Justice entails receiving what we in fact deserve; we did in fact know better. Mercy is not receiving what we in truth deserve.

To be punished, however severely, because we indeed *deserve* it, as C.S. Lewis observed, is to be treated with dignity as human beings created in the image of God. Conversely, to abandon the criteria of righteous and just punishment, as Lewis also pointed out, is to abandon *all* criteria for punishment. Indeed, I am coming to see that mercy extended to offenders whose guilt is certain yet simply ignored creates a moral travesty which, over time, helps pave the way for collapse of the entire social order. This is essentially the argument of Romans 13. Romans 12 concludes with an apostolic proscription of personal retribution, yet St. Paul immediately follows this with a divinely instituted prescription for punishing moral evil. It is for eminently social reasons that "the authorities" are to wield the sword, the *ius gladii* [law of the sword]: due to human depravity and the need for moral-social order the civil magistrate punishes criminal behavior. The implication of Romans 13 is that by *not* punishing moral evil the authorities are not performing their God-appointed responsibility in society. Paul's teaching in Romans 13 squares with his personal experience. Testifying before Festus, the Apostle certifies: "If . . . I am guilty of doing anything deserving death, I do not refuse to die."

## Some Criminals Deserve the Death Penalty

Perhaps the emotional event that pushed me over the (philosophical) edge was the John Wayne Gacy case in 1994. [Gacy was convicted in 1980 of torturing and murdering thirty-three young men and boys.] I visited him on death row. During our hour-long conversation he was totally unrepentant; in fact, he was arrogant. He insisted that he was a Christian, that he believed in Christ, yet he showed not a hint of remorse. The testimony in the trial, of course, was overwhelming. I don't think anybody could possibly believe that he did not commit those crimes, and the crimes were unspeakably barbaric.

What I realized in the days prior to Gacy's execution was that there was simply no other appropriate response than execution if justice was to be served. There are some cases like this—the 1995 Oklahoma federal building bombing a case in point—when no other response is appropriate, no other punishment sufficient for the deliberate savagery of the crime.

The issue in my mind boils down ultimately to just deserts. Indeed, just punishment is a thread running throughout the whole of biblical revelation. Moreover, there is divinely instituted tension that exists between mercy and justice—a tension that, ethically speaking, may *not* be eradicated. Mercy without justice makes a mockery of the sacrifice of the Lamb of God. It ignores the fundamental truth of biblical anthropology: the soul that sins must die; sin incurs a debt that must be paid. Punitive dealings provide a necessary atonement and restore the moral balance that has been disturbed by sin. Purification, one of the most central of biblical themes, reveals to us both the temporal and eternal perspectives on mankind. Purification comes by way of suffering; it prepares the individual to meet his maker. God's redemptive response to the sin dilemma did not—and does not—eradicate the need to bear the consequences of our actions. Which leads me to a second observation.

Reprinted by permission of Chuck Asay and Creators Syndicate.

The death penalty ultimately confronts us with the issue of moral accountability in the present life. Contemporary society seems totally unwilling to assign moral responsibility to anyone. Everything imaginable is due to a dysfunctional family or to having had our knuckles rapped while we were in grade school. Ours is a day in which "abuse excuses" have proliferated beyond our wildest dreams. . . .

Non-Christians and Christians alike are not absolved from the consequences of their behavior. Whether or not faith is professed, penalties for everything from speeding to strangulation apply to all. In American society today, people are literally getting away with murder, and the moral stupor that has descended over our culture reflects a decay, an utter erosion, of time-tested moral norms—norms that have guarded generation after generation. Can anyone really wonder why evidence of a moral dry rot is everywhere?

I come to this view with something of a heavy heart, as some of the most blessed brothers I've known in my Christian walk were on death row. I think of Richard Moore in particular and, of course, Rusty Woomer, about whom I've written in *The Body*. I think of Bob Williams in Nebraska and Johnny Cockrum in Texas.

I have a heavy heart as well because I do not believe the system administers criminal justice fairly. It is merely symbolic justice to execute twenty-five people a year when two thousand are sentenced. (Obviously, the system needs to be thoroughly revamped. Nevertheless, revamping the system, in order that punishment be both *swift and proportionate*, would accord with biblical guidelines and demands the Christian's engagement.) But in spite of the flaws of the system, I have come to believe that God in fact requires capital justice, at least in the case of premeditated murder where there is no doubt of the offender's guilt. This is, after all, *the one* crime in the Bible for which no restitution was possible. Lest we believe the Old Testament was characterized by indiscriminate capital justice, Old Testament law painstakingly distinguished between premeditated murder and involuntary manslaughter; hence, the function of the cities of refuge. Israel's elders, we can be assured, would have adjudicated well at the gate. In the case of involuntary manslaughter, deliverance out of the hand of the avenger occurred. In the case of murder, the convicted criminal was put to death.

## The Death Penalty and Deterrence

Personally, I still doubt that the death-penalty is a general deterrent—and strong evidence exists that it is not likely to be a deterrent when it is so seldom invoked. But I have a hard time escaping the attitude of the biblical writers, that judgment—both temporal and eschatological—is a *certain* reality for those who disobey or reject God's authority. We'll never know how many potential murderers are deterred by the threat of a death penalty, just as we will never know how many lives may be saved by it. But at the bare minimum, it may deter a convict sentenced to life from killing a prison guard or another convict. (In such a case no other punishment is appropriate because all lesser punishments have been exhausted.) And it will certainly prevent a convicted murderer from murdering again. In this regard, I find wisdom in the words of John Stuart Mill:

> As for what is called the failure of death punishment, who is able to judge of that? We partly know who those are whom it has not deterred; but who is there who knows whom it has

deterred, or how many human beings it has saved who would have lived to be murderers if that awful association had not been thrown round the idea of murder from their earliest infancy?

So in spite of my misgivings, I've come to see capital punishment as an essential element of justice. On the whole, the full range of biblical data weighs in its favor. Society should not execute capital offenders merely for the sake of revenge, rather to balance the scales of moral justice which have been disturbed. The death penalty is warranted and should be implemented *only* in those cases where evidence is certain, in accordance with the biblical standard and where no other punishment can satisfy the demands of justice.

## The Sacredness of Human Life

In the public debate over the death penalty, we are dealing with values of the highest order: respect for the sacredness of human life and its protection, the preservation of order in society, and the attainment of justice through law. The function of biblical sanctions against a heinous crime such as murder is to *discourage* the wanton destruction of *innocent* life. Undergirding the biblical sanctions against murder is the utter sacred character of human life. The shedding of blood in ancient Israel polluted the land—a pollution for which there was no substitute— and thus required the death penalty. This is the significance of the sanctions in Genesis 9 against those who would shed the blood of another. It is because humans are created in the image of God that capital punishment for premeditated murder was to be a perpetual obligation. To kill a person was tantamount to killing God in effigy. The Noahic covenant recorded in Genesis 9 antedates Israel and the Mosaic code; it transcends Old Testament law per se and mirrors ethical legislation that is binding for all cultures and eras. The sanctity of human life is rooted in the universal creation ethic and thus retains its force in society. Any culture that fails to distinguish between the criminal and the punitive act, in my opinion, is a culture that cannot survive.

In this way, then, my own ethical thinking has evolved. I'm well aware that sincere Christians stand on both sides of this issue. One's views on the death penalty are by no means a test of fellowship. While we take no pleasure in defining the contours of this difficult ethical issue, the Christian community nevertheless is called upon to articulate standards of biblical justice, even when this may be unpopular. Capital justice, I have come to believe, is part of that nonnegotiable standard. A moral obligation requires civil government to punish crime, and consequently, to enforce capital punishment, albeit under highly restricted conditions.

*"The death penalty cannot be administered in accord with our Constitution."*

# The Death Penalty Is Legally Unjust

Harry A. Blackmun

In 1972, the U.S. Supreme Court found that death sentences were being imposed unfairly and inconsistently; it therefore ruled that then-existing death penalty laws were unconstitutional. In 1976, however, the Court approved newly written laws that clearly defined which crimes deserved to be punished with death. In the following viewpoint, Harry A. Blackmun contends that the attempt to consistently impose the death penalty for the most heinous crimes conflicts with the requirement to consider every case individually. He argues that because these two legal principles cannot be reconciled under the Constitution, capital punishment should be abandoned. Blackmun retired as a justice of the Supreme Court in April 1994.

As you read, consider the following questions:

1. In Blackmun's opinion, what must a death penalty scheme allow in order to be fair?
2. What is required if the death penalty is to be consistent, according to the author?
3. What does the author say is the proper course for the Court when faced with competing constitutional rules?

Excerpted from Harry A. Blackmun's dissenting opinion to the U.S. Supreme Court's order *Callins v. Collins*, no. 93-7054.

*Following are excerpts from Justice Harry A. Blackmun's opinion dissenting from the Supreme Court's order denying review in a Texas death penalty case. The order,* Callins v. Collins, *was unsigned and was issued without an opinion.*

Bruce Edwin Callins will be executed by the State of Texas [Callins received a stay of execution in March 1994 and as of spring 1996 is awaiting a review of his case]. Intravenous tubes attached to his arms will carry the instrument of death, a toxic fluid designed specifically for the purpose of killing human beings. The witnesses, standing a few feet away, will behold Callins, no longer a defendant, an appellant or a petitioner, but a man, strapped to a gurney, and seconds away from extinction

Within days, or perhaps hours, the memory of Callins will begin to fade. The wheels of justice will churn again, and somewhere, another jury or another judge will have the unenviable task of determining whether some human being is to live or die.

We hope, of course, that the defendant whose life is at risk will be represented by competent counsel, someone who is inspired by the awareness that a less-than-vigorous defense truly could have fatal consequences for the defendant. We hope that the attorney will investigate all aspects of the case, follow all evidentiary and procedural rules, and appear before a judge who is still committed to the protection of defendants' rights even now, as the prospect of meaningful judicial oversight has diminished. In the same vein, we hope that the prosecution, in urging the penalty of death, will have exercised its discretion wisely, free from bias, prejudice or political motive, and will be humbled, rather than emboldened, by the awesome authority conferred by the State.

### Fairness vs. Consistency in Death Sentences

But even if we can feel confident that these actors will fulfill their roles to the best of their human ability, our collective conscience will remain uneasy. Twenty years have passed since this Court declared that the death penalty must be imposed fairly, and with reasonable consistency or not at all (see *Furman v. Georgia,* 1972), and, despite the effort of the states and courts to devise legal formulas and procedural rules to meet this daunting challenge, the death penalty remains fraught with arbitrariness, discrimination, caprice and mistake.

This is not to say that the problems with the death penalty today are identical to those that were present twenty years ago. Rather, the problems that were pursued down one hole with procedural rules and verbal formulas have come to the surface somewhere else, just as virulent and pernicious as they were in their original form. Experience has taught us that the constitutional goal of eliminating arbitrariness and discrimination from the administration of death . . . can never be achieved without compromising an equally essential component of fundamental fairness: individualized sentencing. (See *Lockett v. Ohio*, 1978.)

U.S. SUPREME COURT'S DEATH ROW

It is tempting, when faced with conflicting constitutional commands, to sacrifice one for the other or to assume that an acceptable balance between them already has been struck. In the context of the death penalty, however, such jurisprudential maneuvers are wholly inappropriate. The death penalty must be imposed "fairly, and with reasonable consistency, or not at all." (*Eddings v. Oklahoma*, 1982.)

To be fair, a capital sentencing scheme must treat each person convicted of a capital offense with that "degree of respect due the uniqueness of the individual. . . ." That means affording the sentencer the power and discretion to grant mercy in a particular case, and providing avenues for the consideration of any and all relevant mitigating evidence that would justify a sentence less than death.

Reasonable consistency, on the other hand, requires that the death penalty be inflicted evenhandedly, in accordance with reason and objective standards, rather than by whim, caprice or prejudice.

## Judicial Review of Death Sentences Is Vital

Finally, because human error is inevitable and because our criminal justice system is less than perfect, searching appellate review of death sentences and their underlying convictions is a prerequisite to a constitutional death penalty scheme.

On their face, these goals of individual fairness, reasonable consistency and absence of error appear to be attainable: Courts are in the very business of erecting procedural devices from which fair, equitable and reliable outcomes are presumed to flow. Yet, in the death penalty area, this Court, in my view, has engaged in a futile effort to balance these constitutional demands, and now is retreating not only from the *Furman* promise of consistency and rationality, but from the requirement of individualized sentencing as well.

Having virtually conceded that both fairness and rationality cannot be achieved in the administration of the death penalty (*McCleskey v. Kemp*, 1987), the Court has chosen to deregulate the entire enterprise, replacing, it would seem, substantive constitutional requirements with mere aesthetics, and abdicating its statutorily and constitutionally imposed duty to provide meaningful judicial oversight to the administration of death by the states.

From this day forward, I no longer shall tinker with the machinery of death. For more than twenty years I have endeavored—indeed, I have struggled, along with a majority of this Court—to develop procedural and substantive rules that would lend more than the mere appearance of fairness to the death penalty endeavor. . . . Rather than continue to coddle the Court's delusion that the desired level of fairness has been achieved and the need for regulation eviscerated, I feel morally and intellectually obligated simply to concede that the death penalty experiment has failed. It is virtually self-evident to me now that no combination of procedural rules or substantive regulations ever can save the death penalty from its inherent constitutional deficiencies. The basic question—does the system accurately and consistently determine which defendants "deserve" to die?—cannot be answered in the affirmative. . . . The problem is that the inevitability of factual, legal and moral error gives us a system that we know must wrongly kill some defendants, a system that fails to deliver the fair, consistent and reliable sentences of death required by the Constitution. . . .

## Defining Who Deserves Death

There is little doubt now that *Furman's* essential holding was correct. Although most of the public seems to desire, and the Constitution appears to permit, the penalty of death, it surely is beyond dispute that if the death penalty cannot be administered consistently and rationally, it may not be administered at all. . . .

Delivering on the *Furman* promise, however, has proved to be another matter. *Furman* aspired to eliminate the vestiges of racism and the effects of poverty in capital sentencing; it deplored the "wanton" and "random" infliction of death by a government with constitutionally limited power. *Furman* demanded that the sentencer's discretion be directed and limited by procedural rules and objective standards in order to minimize the risk of arbitrary and capricious sentences of death.

In the years following *Furman*, serious efforts were made to comply with its mandate. State legislatures and appellate courts struggled to provide judges and juries with sensible and objective guidelines for determining who should live and who should die. Some states attempted to define who is "deserving" of the death penalty through the use of carefully chosen adjectives, reserving the death penalty for those who commit crimes that are "especially heinous, atrocious or cruel," or "wantonly vile, horrible or inhuman." Other states enacted mandatory death penalty statutes, reading *Furman* as an invitation to eliminate sentencer discretion altogether. . . .

Unfortunately, all this experimentation and ingenuity yielded little of what *Furman* demanded. It soon became apparent that discretion could not be eliminated from capital sentencing without threatening the fundamental fairness due a defendant when life is at stake. Just as contemporary society was no longer tolerant of the random or discriminatory infliction of the penalty of death . . . evolving standards of decency required due consideration of the uniqueness of each individual defendant when imposing society's ultimate penalty.

## Fairness and Consistency Cannot Be Balanced

This development in the American conscience would have presented no constitutional dilemma if fairness to the individual could be achieved without sacrificing the consistency and rationality promised in *Furman*. But over the past two decades, efforts to balance these competing constitutional commands have been to no avail. Experience has shown that the consistency and rationality promised in *Furman* are inversely related to the fairness owed the individual when considering a sentence of death. A step toward consistency is a step away from fairness. . . .

While one might hope that providing the sentencer with as much relevant mitigating evidence as possible will lead to more rational and consistent sentences, experience has taught otherwise. It seems that the decision whether a human being should live or die is so inherently subjective, rife with all of life's understandings, experiences, prejudices and passions, that it inevitably defies the rationality and consistency required by the Constitution. . . .

The consistency promised in *Furman* and the fairness to the individual demanded in *Lockett* are not only inversely related, but irreconcilable in the context of capital punishment. Any statute or procedure that could effectively eliminate arbitrariness from the administration of death would also restrict the sentencer's discretion to such an extent that the sentencer would be unable to give full consideration to the unique characteristics of each defendant and the circumstances of the offense.

By the same token, any statute or procedure that would provide the sentencer with sufficient discretion to consider fully and act upon the unique circumstances of each defendant would "thro(w) open the back door to arbitrary and irrational sentencing.". . .

In my view, the proper course when faced with irreconcilable constitutional commands is not to ignore one or the other, nor to pretend that the dilemma does not exist, but to admit the futility of the effort to harmonize them. This means accepting the fact that the death penalty cannot be administered in accord with our Constitution. . . .

Perhaps one day this Court will develop procedural rules or verbal formulas that actually will provide consistency, fairness and reliability in a capital-sentencing scheme. I am not optimistic that such a day will come. I am more optimistic, though, that this Court eventually will conclude that the effort to eliminate arbitrariness while preserving fairness "in the infliction of (death) is so plainly doomed to failure that it and the death penalty must be abandoned altogether." (*Godfrey v. Georgia*, 1980. . . .) I may not live to see that day, but I have faith that eventually it will arrive. The path the Court has chosen lessens us all.

*"[The Constitution] clearly permits the death
penalty to be imposed."*

# The Death Penalty
# Is Legally Just

Antonin Scalia

In 1972, the U.S. Supreme Court ruled that capital punishment
would be permissible only if it could be applied consistently for
the most heinous crimes. In other rulings, however, the Court
decided that judges and juries must have unlimited power to extend mercy to criminals during sentencing. In the following
viewpoint, Antonin Scalia maintains that capital punishment is
clearly permitted by the Fifth Amendment, but he admits that
these two rulings produce a conflict when attempting to impose
death sentences fairly and consistently. He argues that the contradiction between the rulings does not prove that the death
penalty is unjust but rather that one of the decisions must be
wrong. Scalia is an associate justice of the Supreme Court.

As you read, consider the following questions:

1. According to Scalia, on what basis does Justice Blackmun
   oppose the death penalty?
2. In the author's opinion, on what should Supreme Court
   decisions about the death penalty be based?
3. What conclusion should be drawn when Supreme Court
   decisions are irreconcilable, according to the author?

Excerpted from Antonin Scalia's concurring opinion to the U.S. Supreme Court's order
*Callins v. Collins*, no. 93-7054.

The petition for a writ of certiorari [judicial review] is denied in the case of *Callins v. Collins*, a Texas death penalty case.

Justice Antonin Scalia, concurring.

Justice Harry A. Blackmun dissents from the denial of certiorari in this case with a statement explaining why the death penalty "as currently administered" is contrary to the Constitution of the United States. That explanation often refers to "intellectual, moral and personal" perceptions, but never to the text and tradition of the Constitution. It is the latter rather than the former that ought to control. The Fifth Amendment provides that "[n]o person shall be held to answer for a capital . . . crime, unless on a presentment or indictment of a Grand Jury, . . . nor be deprived of life . . . without due process of law." This clearly permits the death penalty to be imposed, and establishes beyond doubt that the death penalty is not one of the "cruel and unusual punishments" prohibited by the Eighth Amendment.

## Imposing Death vs. Extending Mercy

As Justice Blackmun describes, however, over the years since 1972 this Court has attached to the imposition of the death penalty two quite incompatible sets of commands: the sentencer's discretion to impose death must be closely confined (see *Furman v. Georgia*, 1972), but the sentencer's discretion *not* to impose death (to extend mercy) must be unlimited (see *Eddings v. Oklahoma*, 1982; *Lockett v. Ohio*, 1978). These commands were invented without benefit of any textual or historical support; they are the product of just such "intellectual, moral, and personal" perceptions as Justice Blackmun expresses today, some of which (those that have been "perceived" simultaneously by five members of the Court) have been made part of what is called "the Court's Eighth Amendment jurisprudence."

Though Justice Blackmun joins those of us who have acknowledged the incompatibility of the Court's *Furman* and *Lockett-Eddings* lines of jurisprudence, he unfortunately draws the wrong conclusion from the acknowledgment. He says:

> [T]he proper course when faced with irreconcilable constitutional commands is not to ignore one or the other, nor to pretend that the dilemma does not exist, but to admit the futility of the effort to harmonize them. This means accepting the fact that the death penalty cannot be administered in accord with our Constitution.

Surely a different conclusion commends itself—to wit, that at least one of these judicially announced irreconcilable commands which cause the Constitution to prohibit what its text explicitly permits must be wrong.

Convictions in opposition to the death penalty are often passionate and deeply held. That would be no excuse for reading

## Conflicting Judgments

Justice Harry A. Blackmun finds incompatible two lines of reasoning found in the capital punishment cases the court has decided since *Furman v. Georgia*, 1972. On the one hand, those cases require that a jury's discretion to impose the death penalty must be closely confined in order to eliminate arbitrariness and prejudice in its administration. The idea here is to make sure that the death penalty is meted out for the same kind of heinous crimes. On the other hand, those cases require that a jury have unlimited discretion to consider any evidence a death penalty defendant might wish to offer in his own behalf. This requirement means that a jury might undo what under a constitutional death-penalty statute it otherwise properly would do. . . .

Blackmun argues in *Callins* that the court should "admit the futility of the efforts to harmonize" the two "irreconcilable constitutional commands" and accept "the fact that the death penalty cannot be administered in accord with our Constitution."

Justice Antonin Scalia admits this futility, too, but unlike Blackmun he asks whether the commands are in fact constitutional. For Scalia, something must be wrong with a conclusion (the death penalty is unconstitutional) so plainly at odds with what the text of the Constitution clearly provides. . . .

One would think that in any contest between the Constitution and something else, a judge would side with the Constitution.

Terry Eastland, *American Spectator*, April/May 1994.

---

them into a Constitution that does not contain them, even if they represented the convictions of a majority of Americans. Much less is there any excuse for using that course to thrust a minority's views upon the people. Justice Blackmun begins his statement by describing with poignancy the death of a convicted murderer by lethal injection. He chooses, as the case in which to make that statement, one of the less brutal of the murders that regularly come before us—the murder of a man ripped by a bullet suddenly and unexpectedly, with no opportunity to prepare himself and his affairs, and left to bleed to death on the floor of a tavern. The death-by-injection which Justice Blackmun describes looks pretty desirable next to that. It looks even better next to some of the other cases currently before us which Justice Blackmun did not select as the vehicle for his announcement that the death penalty is always unconstitutional—for example, the case of the eleven-year-old girl raped by four men and then killed by stuffing her panties down her throat. How enviable a quiet death by lethal injection compared with that! If the people conclude that such more brutal deaths may be deterred by capital punishment; indeed, if they merely conclude that justice requires such brutal deaths to be avenged by capital punishment; the creation of false, untextual and unhistorical contradictions within "the Court's Eighth Amendment jurisprudence" should not prevent them.

*"We know of nearly two dozen cases in the twentieth century where the evidence . . . suggests that the wrong person was convicted of murder or rape, sentenced to death, and executed."*

# Innocent People Have Been Executed

Michael L. Radelet, Hugo Adam Bedau, and Constance E. Putnam

Death penalty opponents claim that because the criminal justice system often convicts innocent people, there is a danger that an innocent person will be executed. In the following viewpoint, Michael L. Radelet, Hugo Adam Bedau, and Constance E. Putnam examine the case of James Adams, executed in Florida in 1984, and find evidence that he was innocent. The authors argue that there is evidence that innocent defendants were convicted in 416 capital crime cases in the twentieth century. Twenty-three of these cases, the authors maintain, resulted in the execution of an innocent person. Radelet is a professor of sociology at the University of Florida. Bedau is a professor of philosophy at Tufts University in Medford, Massachusetts. Putnam is a writer.

As you read, consider the following questions:

1. According to Bedau, Radelet, and Putnam, why is it impossible to resolve questions of innocence once defendants have been executed?
2. What types of evidence are included by the authors in their category of official judgments of error?
3. What types of evidence are included by the authors in the category of unofficial judgments?

From *In Spite of Innocence: Erroneous Convictions in Capital Cases* by Michael L. Radelet, Hugo Adam Bedau, and Constance E. Putnam. Copyright 1992 by Michael L. Radelet, Hugo Adam Bedau, and Constance E. Putnam. Reprinted with the permission of the authors and Northeastern University Press.

On May 10, 1984, James Adams was executed in Florida for murder. (As Adams was being executed in the electric chair in Florida State Prison and as death penalty opponents stood in silent vigil across the street, an unidentified man drove by in a pickup truck, and with a thumbs-up gesture shouted, "Fry the nigger!") No national publicity surrounded this case, which had stretched out over a decade. It had begun on the morning of November 12, 1973, with the murder of Edgar Brown in Ft. Pierce, Florida. Brown was found badly beaten, allegedly during the course of a robbery in his home. A sixty-one-year-old rancher and former deputy sheriff, Brown died the next day. Adams was promptly arrested, tried, and convicted. . . .

## Details of the Crime

The killer had entered Edgar Brown's unoccupied home on the morning of November 12, 1973. Sometime later Brown returned home, where he was attacked and beaten with a fireplace poker. Adams's car had been parked in the driveway, and it was seen traveling to and from the victim's home. One witness, Willie Orange, positively identified Adams as the driver of the car; a second witness, John Thompkins, "thought" Adams was the driver. The car was located later that day at a shop where it had been left for the repainting job Adams had been planning for months. Adams claimed his car had been driven that morning, at 10:00 or 10:15 A.M. (one half hour before the assault) by a friend, Vivian Nickerson, and another man, Kenneth Crowell. According to Adams, while they were off in his car—precisely at the time of the homicide—he was at the Nickerson home playing cards.

The victim, it was known, always carried between $700 and $1500 in cash; no cash was found in his wallet after the assault. When Adams was arrested, he had only $185 with him. He also had a credible explanation for the source of this money: His employer had recently lent him $200. The State offered no explanation of what it thought had happened to the other $500 to $1300 that Brown would have been carrying and that had in all likelihood been taken by his killer. One bill in Adams's possession had a dried patch of O-positive blood on it, consistent with the blood of the victim—and that of 45 percent of the rest of the population.

The one person who had a chance to identify the killer at Brown's home was Foy Hortman. He testified that he drove up to the house shortly after Brown had returned home and heard a woman shout from inside, "In the name of God, don't do it!" He then saw and briefly spoke with someone leaving the house, but failed to identify Adams as that person. More than that, he testified that the person he spoke with was blacker than Adams and, unlike Adams, had no mustache. On the day of the homicide, Hortman viewed a police line-up that included Adams and said he was positive that none of the men was the person he had seen leaving the Brown house. Nonetheless, at trial Hortman testified that Adams "may or may not have been" the person at the scene. (A logician would call that remark a tautology, but the jury appears to have been influenced by it.)

## Witnesses Against Adams

John Thompkins testified that he thought it was James Adams he had seen driving a car to the victim's home shortly before the homicide. "It had to be [Adams]," Thompkins said, "because he throwed up his hand at me, because everybody that passed there don't hardly wave at you unless you know him." Not a very precise or damning statement, yet the State relied heavily on it.

---

### The Case of Jesse Tafero

In Florida, Sonia Jacobs and Jesse Tafero were convicted of murdering a state trooper and his companion in 1976 and were sentenced to death. The chief evidence against them was supplied by the third person at the scene of the crime, an ex-convict named Walter Rhodes. In exchange for his testimony, Rhodes pleaded guilty to second-degree murder and received a life sentence.

In 1981 Jacobs's death sentence was reduced to life imprisonment. But in 1990 Tafero—despite his protestations of innocence—was executed. Micki Dickoff, a childhood friend of Jacobs's, read about Tafero's execution and re-established contact with Jacobs. Thanks to Dickoff's unflagging efforts, federal courts threw out Jacobs's conviction; in 1992 she was released when the state admitted not having the evidence to retry her. It now appears Jacobs was completely innocent. Why is the Jacobs-Tafero case so significant? If Jacobs was innocent, then the execution of Tafero was probably the execution of an innocent man, because the same evidence (later shown to be insufficient) used to convict Jacobs had also been used to convict Tafero. The information that freed her would have freed him—if he had not already been executed.

Michael L. Radelet, Hugo Adam Bedau, Constance E. Putnam, *In Spite of Innocence,* 1994.

---

Willie Orange, on the other hand, did positively identify Adams as driving the car away from the Brown home. His was the sole testimony that placed Adams near the crime scene. Perhaps not so incidentally, it later turned out that Orange believed Adams was having an affair with his wife. During the clemency hearing, three witnesses were located who had heard Orange stating before the trial that he was going to testify against

Adams because of this affair. One witness quoted Orange as saying before the trial, "I'm going to send him [Adams] because he's been going with my wife." A polygraph administered to Orange to support Adams's appeal for clemency in 1984, while hardly conclusive, indicated that Orange was being deceptive when he testified at the trial.

Vivian Nickerson, the person Adams said had access to his car at the time of the homicide, was fifteen years old. She was very large for her age and had a strikingly masculine appearance. In fact, she resembled James Adams, and her height, size, and complexion fit Hortman's eyewitness description better than Adams's did. It is possible that she was the person Hortman saw leaving the victim's house. If she was, that would explain another loose end not tied up by the State's theory of the crime: Hers could have been the woman's voice Hortman testified he had heard coming from inside the house. Yet no photos of Vivian Nickerson were shown to Hortman, and he never saw her in a police line-up.

Interestingly enough, Nickerson was called by Adams to corroborate his alibi at trial. She was a reluctant witness, however, and ended up hurting his case. By claiming that he had not arrived at her house until 11:00 A.M., she undermined his testimony. In a pretrial deposition, given under oath, she had stated that Adams reached her house prior to 10:30 and that she had then borrowed his car. In other words, contrary to what she claimed during the trial, Nickerson when deposed had said that Adams was at her house and that she was driving his car at the time of the crime. This inconsistency was by no means a minor one; unfortunately, Adams's defense counsel never confronted Nickerson with the contradiction.

### Additional Reasons to Doubt Adams's Guilt

The most significant blow to the State's case against Adams arose from evidence not presented at trial. En route to the hospital in an ambulance with her husband, Mrs. Brown found strands of hair clasped in his hand—hair presumably pulled from the head of his assailant. The State's crime laboratory compared these hairs with samples of Adams's hair and determined that although the hair was "very dark brown, Negroid, [and] curly," Adams was definitely not its source. This report, however, was not released until three days after Adams had been sentenced. Even then, when it could have been used to support a request for a new trial, it was not given to the defense attorneys.

In their 1984 clemency papers, Adams's attorneys succinctly stated their case as follows:

> In sum, had all of the evidence raising doubt about Mr. Adams's guilt been submitted to the jury, there would have been at least

a reasonable doubt about Mr. Adams's guilt. The evidence would have shown that the only person who had an opportunity to observe the perpetrator was "positive" that Mr. Adams was not that person. The evidence would have shown that Willie Orange's identification of Mr. Adams as the person driving away from Brown's house was wholly unbelievable because of his stated motive to "get" James Adams. The evidence would have shown that a specimen of hair asserted by the investigating deputy to have been recovered from the hand of Mr. Brown in the ambulance after the assault against him could not have come from James Adams. . . . Had the jury been told about Vivian Nickerson's sworn testimony less than two months before James Adams's trial which unequivocally corroborated Mr. Adams's testimony that he was continuously at Ms. Nickerson's house from before the homicide until well after the homicide, the jury would have been more likely to suspect Vivian Nickerson as the perpetrator than James Adams.

## Questions of Innocence After Death Are Moot

No doubt due process of law failed rather badly in the Adams case, and these deficiencies played a critical role in his conviction and death sentence. But was Adams truly innocent? Did he deserve to be acquitted on the ground that he had no involvement in the murder of Edgar Brown, even though members of the trial jury—given the evidence before them—believed otherwise? Adams's postconviction attorneys, Richard Burr and Craig Barnard, thought so. We think so. But from the moment Adams was executed, it became virtually impossible to resolve the issue one way or the other. There is no legal forum in which the innocence of the dead can be officially confirmed, or even satisfactorily investigated. The court of public opinion—such as it is—is the only recourse, and James Adams was too obscure, too bereft of friends and supporters with time and money, to have his claim of innocence tested and vindicated posthumously in that forum.

Once Adams was dead, his attorneys had to turn their full attention to the plight of other death row clients. Time spent re-investigating the circumstances of the Edgar Brown murder in the hope of vindicating the late James Adams was time denied to clients still alive but facing the electric chair. No newspaper editor or team of reporters, no investigative journalist, has seen fit (so far as we know) to re-open the Adams case. Instead, a giant question mark continues to haunt his execution, a question mark that will probably never be removed. A rare case? Perhaps, but not unique. We know of nearly two dozen cases in the twentieth century where the evidence similarly suggests that the wrong person was convicted of murder or rape, sentenced to death, and executed. . . .

There are hundreds of other cases in which innocent persons

were convicted of a capital (or potentially capital) crime but were then fortunate enough to have their innocence established, thus saving them from a lifetime behind bars or, worse, an execution. . . .

We have identified 416 cases in which the wrong person was convicted of murder (or of capital rape and then sentenced to death) in the United States so far in the twentieth century. All together, roughly a third of the defendants in these cases were not merely convicted, but also sentenced to death.

---

## Irrefutable Evidence of Innocent Death Row Prisoners

It is now irrefutable that innocent persons are still being sentenced to death, and the chances are high that innocent persons have been or will be executed.

No issue posed by capital punishment is more disturbing to the public than the prospect that the government might execute an innocent person. A 1993 national poll found that the number one concern raising doubts among voters regarding the death penalty is the danger of a mistaken execution. Fifty-eight percent of voters are disturbed that death penalty practices might allow an innocent person to be executed.

On July 23, 1993, the House Subcommittee on Civil and Constitutional Rights heard testimony from four men who were released from prison after serving years on death row—living proof that innocent people are sentenced to death.

House Committee on the Judiciary, *Innocence and the Death Penalty*, November 1994.

---

Knowing the kind of crime and the kind of error we are interested in does not, by itself, tell us whether a given case really involves a miscarriage of justice. To make that decision, we have relied on *evidence* that falls into two categories. The more important kind of evidence is *official judgments of error*. (About 90 percent of the cases belong to this category.) Such judgments can take several different forms, and they can be delivered by any of the three branches of government. They may be found in a commutation or a pardon, or in the award of an indemnity to the convicted defendant after release (by special act of the legislature, or after litigation in the courts). They may take the form of a reversal of the criminal conviction by an appellate court, followed by a further judgment: a prosecutor's decision not to seek another trial for the defendant, a jury's decision to acquit at retrial, a judge's directed verdict of acquittal. Obviously, the more of these official actions there are in a given case, the more complete is the evidence of official belief in the defendant's innocence—and, to that extent, the more compelling the inference that the defendant really is innocent.

The second category of evidence consists of *unofficial judgments*. There is no limit to the variety of this kind of evidence. The following examples are typical but by no means exhaustive: The supposed crime turns out never to have taken place at all, even though the jury thought otherwise; the real culprit confesses or is identified but never arrested, indicted, or convicted; a state official (such as a prison warden) investigates the case and concludes that the courts were wrong and that the convicted defendant really is innocent—but no extrajudicial official action comes to the defendant's aid; the defendant's attorney or family uncovers crucial evidence showing that the defendant is innocent, but cannot convince any court or official body (as happened in the James Adams case). Or perhaps other students of the case, journalists or scholars, re-examine all the available evidence and conclude that the defendant cannot be guilty.

### Execution of Innocents

These are the sorts of evidence that led to our judgment that miscarriages of justice resulting in the execution of the innocent have occurred. To the best of our knowledge, no state or federal officials have ever acknowledged that a wrongful execution has taken place in the twentieth century. . . .

During the twentieth century in the United States, more than seven thousand men and women have been legally executed for capital crimes. Many thousands more have been sentenced to death. Probably a quarter of a million persons have been convicted of criminal homicide. The errors, blunders, and tragedies recounted in this viewpoint barely scratch the surface of this vast output of the nation's criminal justice system. Some of the stories we have rescued from near oblivion, but although our research has often broken new ground, we know that it is far from complete. Hundreds of cases, many of them involving miscarriages of justice every bit as serious as any we describe, almost certainly remain to be investigated. Unknown hundreds of other cases have completely disappeared from sight; we will never know whether justice was done to the defendant. This is especially true of the cases from earlier in the century, or those where the defendant was a member of a repressed minority—a Native American or Hispanic, a recent immigrant, a black. We believe, however, that we have provided a solid base line for future investigations.

*"The Bedau-Radelet study is remarkable not . . . for demonstrating that mistakes involving the death penalty are common, but rather for demonstrating how* uncommon *they are."*

# Innocent People Have Not Been Executed

Stephen Markman

Opponents of the death penalty claim that innocent people have been executed. In the following viewpoint, Stephen Markman examines the evidence presented by death penalty opponents and argues that it does not prove that any innocent defendants have been put to death in twentieth-century America. In the case of James Adams, cited by anti–death penalty researchers, Markman finds the evidence of Adams's guilt overwhelming. Markman is a lawyer in Detroit and a former U.S. assistant attorney general.

As you read, consider the following questions:

1. According to Markman, why do the majority of Americans support the death penalty?
2. Why does the burden of proof lie with those who claim that innocent people have been executed, in the author's opinion?
3. According to the author, what types of evidence do Hugo Adam Bedau and Michael L. Radelet present to show that innocent people have been executed?

Excerpted from Stephen Markman, "Innocents on Death Row?" *National Review*, September 12, 1994; ©1994 by National Review, Inc., 150 E. 35th St., New York, NY 10016. Reprinted by permission.

In announcing that he would "no longer tinker with the machinery of death" by voting to sustain capital punishment, Justice Harry Blackmun relied not only upon an understanding of the Constitution informed more by his own curious conscience than by the text or history of that document but also upon his belief that "innocent persons have been executed . . . and will continue to be executed under our death-penalty scheme."

In making this assertion, Justice Blackmun cited a study published in 1987 in the *Stanford Law Review* by two longtime opponents of capital punishment, Hugo Bedau and Michael Radelet. The authors purported to identify "350 cases in which defendants convicted of capital or potentially capital crimes in this century, and in many cases sentenced to death, have later been found to be innocent." This finding was widely heralded in national press releases issued by the American Civil Liberties Union (ACLU).

Lest such a pseudo-fact gain permanent currency in the capital-punishment debate, Paul Cassell and I, both with the Department of Justice at the time, undertook to study these same cases. Since our findings, also published in the *Stanford Law Review* in 1988, were unaccountably overlooked by Justice Blackmun, I feel compelled to summarize them in order to place the ongoing debate in its proper historical context.

### The Death Penalty Protects Innocent Lives

The danger of executing an innocent person, as well as the uniquely irremediable nature of such a mistake, can hardly be denied by even the most committed proponent of the death penalty. The overwhelming majority of Americans who support the death penalty do not imagine that society is able to administer it with "Godlike perspicacity," in Walter Berns's phrase. Rather, they support it because, through a combination of deterrence, incapacitation, and the imposition of just punishment, the death penalty serves to protect a vastly greater number of innocent lives than are likely to be lost through its erroneous application. Some may further believe that a society would be guilty of a suicidal failure of nerve if it were to forgo the use of an appropriate and deserved punishment simply because it is not humanly possible to eliminate the risk of mistake entirely.

Indeed, the Bedau-Radelet study is remarkable not (as Justice Blackmun seems to believe) for demonstrating that mistakes involving the death penalty are common, but rather for demonstrating how *uncommon* they are. Indeed, to make the finer point, this study—the most thorough and painstaking analysis ever on the subject—fails to prove that a single such mistake has occurred in the United States during the twentieth century.

One cannot state categorically that mistakes never have been made, but the burden properly belongs with those who have endorsed the proposition that innocent persons have been executed with some degree of regularity in this country. Such a burden lies with Justice Blackmun and his allies because in every capital case a unanimous jury of twelve citizens concluded beyond a reasonable doubt that an individual had committed a capital crime, usually first-degree murder. Further, in every one of these cases a trial judge and an assortment of appellate judges concluded both that the trial was fair and that the twelve jurors had acted reasonably in their determination. While such procedures do not give iron-clad assurances that innocent people have not been convicted, they place the burden of proof squarely upon the opposition.

## Deterrent Effect Outweighs the Risks

[Some death penalty supporters] say that even if a few innocent lives are taken, the deterrent effects of the death penalty excuse those risks. Overall, more potential homicides of innocent victims are prevented by the death penalty, they contend, than the number of innocent people who might be wrongfully executed. The American public apparently agrees. According to a June 1995 Gallup poll, 57% of respondents say they would favor the death penalty, even if one out of 100 people sentenced to death were actually innocent.

*Issues and Controversies on File*, December 29, 1995.

Given that the Bedau-Radelet study has been relied upon by a Supreme Court Justice to demonstrate something relevant to the matter of wrongful executions, it does not seem picky to inquire whether or not wrongful executions are anywhere in evidence. The figure of "350" cases (since 1992 increased to 416), which was highlighted by the ACLU in its press releases, does not refer to 350 Americans wrongfully executed. In the majority of these cases, the death penalty either was not available or was not the sentence given. The number includes cases of people who were charged with capital crimes but convicted of lesser offenses, such as second-degree murder or manslaughter; people who were convicted of capital crimes but sentenced to imprisonment rather than death; and people who were convicted of capital crimes but who had their convictions overturned on appeal. Only 200 of the allegedly wrongful convictions in the Bedau-Radelet study involve first-degree murders in which capital punishment was an option, and in only 139 of these 200 cases were the defendants actually sentenced to death. In only 23 of these

139 cases were the death sentences actually carried out.

So, if there were wrongful executions, it is with regard to these twenty-three cases, not with regard to those cases in which, as Bedau and Radelet put it, "relatively adventitious factors" occurred to prevent the execution of allegedly innocent people. But appellate review, the exercise of judicial discretion in sentencing, and legislative decisions not to prescribe capital sanctions for crimes falling short of first-degree murder are not "relatively adventitious factors." Focusing on trial-court dispositions alone completely ignores the procedural protections against erroneous convictions that are built into the system. "Relatively adventitious" factors have, in fact, interceded in 94 per cent of all those cases in which Bedau and Radelet concluded that innocent people were convicted of capital offenses.

## Evidence of Innocence

Thus, only twenty-three of the cited cases are relevant to Justice Blackmun's concerns. What is the standard by which the authors assure us that miscarriages of justice occurred in these cases? Their standard is whether "a majority of neutral observers, given the evidence at [the authors'] disposal, would judge the defendant in question to be innocent." But as they acknowledge, "in none of these cases . . . can we point to the implication of another person or to the confession of the true killer, much less to any official action admitting the execution of an innocent person."

Instead, Bedau and Radelet appear to have scoured defendants' briefs, collected newspaper rumors, transcribed the "unshaken convictions" of defense attorneys, and identified lapses in prosecutorial conduct or trial procedure. On the basis of such evidence, the authors assert their own conclusions that people sentenced to death "have later been found to be innocent" or "proved to be innocent."

## The Case of James Adams

Examination of individual cases cited by the authors will only confirm the reasonableness of the jury's verdict to at least some "neutral observers." Consider, for example, the case of James Adams, one of the twenty-three, who was convicted of first-degree murder and executed in 1984. His case is significant in that it is the only alleged example of an erroneous execution since capital-punishment procedures were radically revamped by the Supreme Court in 1976. Here is the authors' description of the evidence:

> Witnesses located Adams's car at the time of the crime at the home of the victim, a white rancher. Some of the victim's jewelry was found in the car trunk. Adams maintained his inno-

cence, claiming that he had loaned the car to his girlfriend. A witness identified Adams as driving the car away from the victim's home shortly after the crime. This witness, however, was driving a large truck in the direction opposite to Adams and probably could not have had a good look at the driver. It was later discovered that this witness was angry with Adams for allegedly dating his wife. A second witness heard a voice inside the victim's home at the time and saw someone fleeing. He stated this voice was a woman's; the day after the crime he stated that the fleeing person was positively not Adams. More importantly, a hair sample found clutched in the victim's hand, which in all likelihood had come from the assailant, did not match Adams's hair.

Despite being presented with this evidence "a month before Adams's execution," Florida Governor Robert Graham "refused to grant even a short stay so that these questions could be resolved."

This analysis of the Adams trial record, which Justice Blackmun has relied upon in his opposition to the death penalty, seriously distorts and misrepresents the evidence. A more thorough analysis of the testimony reveals the following:

1. The witness driving the truck was able to identify Adams as the driver of the car because the car was weaving so badly that the witness had to pull over to the far side of the road and stop. Indeed, the car came very close to hitting him. The witness identified Adams from a line-up the day after the incident.

2. With respect to Adams's dating the witness's wife, such a theory was raised by the defense counsel in his opening argument. However, no evidence to that effect was ever presented at trial. Indeed, Adams never even raised the issue in his post-trial motions, although it would have been relevant to the witness's credibility.

3. In recalling having heard a "woman's" voice in the house, the second witness was referring to the voice not of the killer but of the person being killed. Furthermore, his general description of the person fleeing the house matched Adams. This witness said only that he could not identify Adams with certainty as the fleeing person, not that it was "positively not Adams."

## Refuting Evidence of Innocence

4. The allegedly exculpatory hair sample was made known to Adams's counsel well before trial. He chose not even to offer it either at trial or on appeal. Most likely, the hair had come from sweepings of the floor of the ambulance carrying the victim to the hospital or from one of several people who attempted to treat the victim's wounds at the death scene, not from the killer's head.

5. Adams's alibi defense was that he was not in the area of the crime on the day of the crime. He was contradicted on this by

three other witnesses who placed him or his car at the scene shortly before the crime. In addition, Adams's own alibi witness contradicted him on his whereabouts at the time of the crime.

6. Several hours after the murder, Adams took his car to a body shop and asked to have it painted a different color.

7. When arrested by police later that day driving a friend's car, Adams had in his possession a twenty-dollar bill stained with blood of the victim's type. When asked about the blood, Adams said that it had come from a cut on his finger. Adams's blood type did not match that on the bill.

8. When arrested, Adams had in his possession his own blood-ied clothing; the blood matched the victim's. He was also found in the possession of jewelry and eyeglasses from the victim's house.

9. In addition, evidence was presented concerning Adams's demeanor following the murder, the circumstance of his having $200 in his possession shortly after having borrowed $35 from two friends, the likelihood that this amount of money in the particular denominations had been in the victim's possession that day, and a series of conflicting statements made by Adams to the police.

All in all, evaluation of the Adams evidence would be likely to persuade few "neutral observers" that the jury had acted unreasonably in determining that Adams was guilty of homicide. Bedau and Radelet give little weight to the considered judgments of juries and judges who have decided and reviewed cases, but it is unclear why the judgments of these particular "neutral observers" are accorded so little deference.

The authors are able to maintain that Adams was a victim of a "miscarriage of justice" only by relying upon a highly skewed picture of the evidence. Moreover, this treatment of the Adams case is not an aberration. Rather, it is systematic throughout their analysis of these instances of allegedly wrongful execution. . . .

## Not Infallible, but . . .

Again, it cannot be disputed that error is possible in the process of imposing any criminal sanctions, including the death penalty. But, where juries and judges have unanimously concluded and repeatedly re-concluded that there is no reasonable doubt of a person's guilt, those who would question these determinations carry the burden of proof.

After "sustained and systematic" research, Bedau and Radelet have pointed to 23 out of more than 7,000 executions during the twentieth century in the United States which they believe to have been erroneous. Presumably, these would be among the most compelling cases for the authors' proposition. Yet in each of the cases where there is a record to review, there are eyewitnesses, confessions, physical evidence, and circumstantial evidence in support of the defendant's guilt. The authors' claims that the defendants were later "found" or "proven" to be innocent are utterly unpersuasive.

Concededly, it can be a difficult task to raise reasonable doubts about guilt in long-forgotten cases, let alone to prove innocence. However, it is Bedau and Radelet who argue that existing law should be changed because of an identifiable harm; accordingly, they bear the burden of producing credible evidence that the harm exists. It is hard to imagine their evidence satisfying such a burden, except for Justice Blackmun.

None of this is to deny the legitimacy of arguments against the death penalty predicated upon moral opposition. Yet these arguments are not at the core of what either Bedau and Radelet or Justice Blackmun argues. Bedau has written elsewhere that it is "false sentimentality to argue that the death penalty ought to be abolished because of the abstract possibility that an innocent person might be executed when the record fails to disclose that such cases occur." Justice Blackmun, too, does not argue in terms of the inevitability of error but rather on the grounds that the present system is incapable of delivering "reliable sentences of death."

While the most inveterate opponents of capital punishment are not influenced by whether or not it is administered in a "reliable" fashion, Bedau and Radelet sought to develop a broader base of opposition to the death penalty. Justice Blackmun, who in the past did not join his former colleagues William Brennan and Thurgood Marshall in moral opposition to capital punishment under all circumstances, reflects this intended audience. Those who look at the Bedau-Radelet study with an open mind, however, will see that it speaks eloquently about the extraordinary rarity of error in capital punishment.

> "However advanced the aesthetics of state death,
> an execution is still a killing, a legal homicide."

# Executions Are Cruel and Inhumane

Nicholas Jenkins

The overwhelming majority of states that have death penalty statutes use lethal injection as the means of execution because it is thought to be a humane form of death. In the following viewpoint, Nicholas Jenkins argues that lethal injection, because it is often botched, is no more humane than any of the other forms of execution—from hanging to electrocution—that society has come to consider cruel and unusual. Jenkins is an art and literature critic and is the author of *The Business of Image: Visualizing the Corporate Message*.

As you read, consider the following questions:

1. When did the world's first electric chair execution take place, according to Jenkins?
2. In how many cases of lethal injection are there likely to be complications, according to the author?
3. In the author's words, why is it often difficult to assess correct dosages for lethal injections?

Conscience argues against its ethos, statistics confirm its racial bias, skepticism revolts from its finality, and economics warns of its costs, yet the death penalty, like some unkillable movie gorgon, keeps coming. To slow its progress, opponents call its social effectiveness a myth. Proponents, although they usually don't come out and say so, know that the mythical, phantasmal aspects of the death penalty are precisely what account for its persistence.

Part of the myth—the symmetrical-justice part—is obvious, even to the convicted. Robert Lowell, imprisoned in 1943 as a conscientious objector, found himself in Manhattan's West Street Jail alongside Louis (Lepke) Buchalter, the boss of Murder, Inc., who was awaiting electrocution. The prospect of the chair, Lowell wrote in a poem, shimmered before the enfeebled gangster like a mysterious gateway back to the violent highs of his youth, "an oasis in his air/of lost connections." For sizable segments of the electorate, too, capital punishment is a mirage promising a return to a more "connected" world—a dream solution to a nightmare of social despair.

### The Search for a Humane Execution Method

In order to survive, the death penalty must adapt to other fantasies as well, prominent among them the wish to kill without making a show of it and without assuming the guilt that comes with inflicting pain. The search for mechanisms that execute cleanly and, by prevailing standards, humanely, which has been going on ever since drawing-and-quartering gave way to the guillotine, continually forces death-penalty enthusiasts to compromise their (demonstrably false) deterrence argument by finding venues that are ever more private and methods that seem ever less overtly cruel.

New York has a special niche in this history. Slightly more than a century ago, the state's governor appointed a panel—popularly known as the Death Commission—to provide him with an acceptable alternative to hanging. (Among the options rejected at the time was lethal injection.) The commission recommended the application of electric current as the most rapid and painless method available. Electricity, the symbol of modern civilization, would dispatch that civilization's irredeemably corrupted elements like a light bulb banishing darkness. The world's first electrocution took place at Auburn State Prison on August 6, 1890. William Kemmler was the convict. In the days before the execution, newspapers hailed the new method as "euthanasia by electricity." (After seeing Kemmler convulsed in the chair, after smelling his burning flesh, and noticing the "purplish foam" that spilled from his mouth, witnesses were less certain.) The man who pulled the switch, Edwin F. Davis, New York's first state electrician, was accounted a gentle soul, dutiful but concerned for the creatures in his care. Davis's hobby was beekeeping—a pastime in which, as a hooded intruder pillaging the hive and suffering the stings of the enraged bee-citizens, he could act out a vivid rite of identification with his prisoners.

---

## Botched Lethal Injections

Randy Woolls, Texas, August 20, 1986:
Woolls, a former drug addict, had to help the execution technicians find a good vein for the lethal injection. . . .

Raymond Landry, Texas, December 14, 1988:
Two minutes into the execution, the syringe came out of Landry's vein, spraying deadly chemicals across the room toward witnesses. The observation curtain was pulled for fourteen minutes while the execution team reinserted the catheter into the vein.

Robyn Lee Parks, Oklahoma, March 10, 1992:
Two minutes after the drugs were administered, the muscles in Parks's jaw, neck, and abdomen began to react spasmodically for approximately forty-five seconds. Parks continued to gasp and violently gag until he died, eleven minutes after the drugs were administered.

Michael L. Radelet, *Harper's Magazine*, June 1995.

---

What could be just barely presented as humane a century ago—and still survives as a method of execution in twelve states—is now widely felt to be repugnant, obsolete, barbarous. To do to animals what is routinely done to people can even be criminal: in California, Cynthia McFadden, of ABC News, reported not long ago, prosecutions are under way against chinchilla ranchers who electrocute their animals. The American Veterinary Medical Association's guidelines for animal euthanasia sternly specify that for a creature to be killed humanely it must be rendered unconscious before it is jolted.

## The Advent of Lethal Injection

As electrocution has lost favor, lethal injection has gained ground. (It is now lawful in twenty-seven states—more than two-thirds of those that execute.) This method, drawing on the iconography of doctorly efficiency, kindness, and discretion, conforms to a national habit of medicalizing everything from laziness to incest. The lethal injection got its biggest public boost from the pioneer of high-tech, clean-war solutions to the nation's military needs. In 1973, when he was governor of California, Ronald Reagan likened executing a criminal with an injection to the best way of dealing with a doomed horse: "You call the veterinarian and the vet gives it a shot and the horse goes to sleep—that's it." Just as external enemies would be fought with lasers and "surgical" strikes, so, under the dispensation of the needle, the internal enemy could be made to glide away as smoothly as King Arthur in his barge, drifting into the mist.

The fact is that lethal injections aren't uncomplicated or foolproof. In roughly one out of four cases, there are likely to be difficulties in locating a vein for the catheter through which a sedative, a paralytic agent, and a heart-stopping chemical must flow into the prisoner's body. When the probing fails, it can be necessary to perform a venous cutdown—a bloody procedure—to make a viable opening. (In 1985, in Texas, it took forty minutes of gurney time to pierce a vein in Stephen Peter Morin's body.) If the catheter misses a vein and instead penetrates subcutaneous tissue—always a possibility, since, despite the aura of medical ceremony surrounding lethal injections, doctors are forbidden to perform them—the sedative may wear off and the prisoner awaken while he or she is suffocating. In addition, just as the length of the drop was always a chancy calculation for the hangman, correct doses are difficult to assess for convicts with serious alcohol or drug histories.

## Executions Are Inhumane

The fantasy that electrocution and, now, injection are steps toward decency remains a powerful one. But what casts this humanitarianism in a different light and reveals the true object of its solicitude is some of the smaller procedures preceding an execution. In the states that electrocute, a prisoner may be invited (or forced) to put on a diaper before leaving the condemned cell for the last time. Muscle spasms mean that convicts usually defecate and urinate while they are in the all-powerful grip of the electric current. This sanitary etiquette has little to do with the needs of the prisoner and much to do with the sensibilities of those who carry out and witness the execution. Even more grotesque morally (because it involves an active denial of what is taking place) is the practice during execution by injection of swabbing the prisoner's forearm, as if to insure that the puncture wound won't become infected. It is hard to avoid the conclusion that an important part of the evolving technology of execution is driven by a need to find a process that seems bland enough to allow the death penalty itself to persist. The methods of execution have as much to do with a wish not to trouble our own tender consciences as with a desire not to cause pain to someone else. . . .

It's a good time to drop the cant about decency and concern.

However advanced the aesthetics of state death, an execution is still a killing, a legal homicide. That fact ought to be faced in all its starkness, not wrapped in a veil of morally neutral, medico-technical mystification. If history is a guide, the lethal injection will look as sickening a hundred years from now as the electric chair does today. Decency will not be served until everyone has come to understand that the only good death-penalty statute is a repealed one.

*"It is in fact possible to conceive of a method of execution that would cause neither pain nor physical trauma, require no medical procedure, . . . and use no hazardous chemicals."*

# Executions Can Be Humane

Stuart A. Creque

In October 1994, a California judge ruled that execution in the gas chamber violated the Eighth Amendment's ban on cruel and unusual punishment. In the following viewpoint, Stuart A. Creque maintains that the forms of execution in use today—firing squad, hanging, and electrocution—could likewise be considered inhumane because each runs a substantial risk that a mishap would result in a gruesome, painful death for the prisoner. He argues that execution by nitrogen asphyxiation would be a completely painless form of execution, eliminating concerns about cruel and unusual punishment. Creque is a freelance writer in Moraga, California.

As you read, consider the following questions:

1. According to Creque, what are the consequences of a botched firing squad execution?
2. What customs have been put in place out of concern for the executioner's conscience, in the author's words?
3. What is the first symptom of nitrogen asphyxiation, according to the author?

Stuart A. Creque, "Killing with Kindness," *National Review*, September 11, 1995; ©1995 by National Review, Inc., 150 E. 35th St., New York, NY 10016. Reprinted by permission.

In October 1994, Judge Marilyn Hall Patel of the Ninth U.S. District Court ruled that execution in California's gas chamber is a form of cruel and unusual punishment, the first ruling ever by a state or federal judge to invalidate a method of execution on Eighth Amendment grounds. She noted that the evidence showed that the condemned man might remain conscious for several minutes, experiencing the emotions of "anxiety, panic, terror," as well as "exquisitely painful muscle spasms" and "intense visceral pain."

## All Executions Involve Trauma

On its face, Judge Patel's ruling applies only to the gas chamber, but every method of execution in current use involves toxic chemicals or physical trauma to induce death—and every method can go awry. An ideal hanging snaps the condemned man's neck cleanly; a botched one either strangles him slowly or severs the head entirely from the body. A firing squad that misses its mark leaves the condemned man conscious as he bleeds to death. In the electric chair, according to eyewitness accounts, some condemned men have literally been cooked until their flesh was charred and loosened from the bone; some had sparks and flame emanating from their cranial-cap electrodes.

Besides society's concern for the condemned man's physical suffering, all of these methods implicitly require an executioner to inflict some degree of trauma upon the condemned. Concern for the executioner's conscience drives such customs as loading one of the guns for a firing squad with a blank cartridge, so that each member of the squad can imagine that his will be the non-lethal shot. And with lethal injection, the executioner's use of skills and procedures normally devoted to lifesaving poses ethical questions for medical caregivers.

Given these defects, abolitionists will presumably press to have each of these methods declared "cruel and unusual." The intended result of these efforts is to make the death penalty unconstitutional in practice, even if it remains constitutional in theory.

It is in fact possible to conceive of a method of execution that would cause neither pain nor physical trauma, require no medical procedure (other than pronouncing death), and use no hazardous chemicals. A case of accidental death suggests such a method.

Early in the Space Shuttle program, a worker at Kennedy Space Center walked into an external fuel tank (a vessel nearly as big inside as a Boeing 737) to inspect it. He was not aware that it had been purged with pure nitrogen gas to prevent oxygen in the air from corroding its interior. Since nitrogen is the major component of ordinary air, pure nitrogen has no distinctive feel, smell, or taste; the worker had no indication that anything was out of the ordinary. After walking a short distance into the tank, he lost consciousness and collapsed. A co-worker, not realizing that his collapse had an external cause, ran in to aid him and succumbed also. By the time other workers realized what was happening, the two men were dead.

## Method of Execution by State

Methods of Execution Permitted

| State | Electrocution | Firing Squad | Gas Chamber | Hanging | Lethal Injection |
|---|---|---|---|---|---|
| Alabama | • | | | | |
| Arizona | | | • | | |
| Arkansas | | | | | • |
| California | | | • | | • |
| Colorado | | | | | • |
| Connecticut | • | | | | |
| Delaware | | | | | • |
| Florida | • | | | | |
| Georgia | • | | | | |
| Idaho | | • | | | • |
| Illinois | | | | | • |
| Indiana | • | | | | |
| Kansas | | | | | • |
| Kentucky | • | | | | |
| Louisiana | | | | | • |
| Maryland | | | • | | |
| Mississippi | | | | | • |
| Missouri | | | | | • |
| Montana | | | | • | • |
| Nebraska | • | | | | |
| Nevada | | | | | • |
| New Hampshire | | | | • | • |
| New Jersey | | | | | • |
| New Mexico | | | | | • |
| New York | | | | | • |
| North Carolina | | | • | | • |
| Ohio | • | | | | • |
| Oklahoma | | | | | • |
| Oregon | | | | | • |
| Pennsylvania | | | | | • |
| South Carolina | • | | | | |
| South Dakota | | | | | • |
| Tennessee | | | | | • |
| Texas | | | | | • |
| Utah | | • | | | • |
| Virginia | • | | | | |
| Washington | | | | • | • |
| Wyoming | | | | | • |

*CQ Researcher*, March 10, 1995.

More recently, a bizarre accident involving nitrogen killed two people in the Bay Area. They had stolen from a hospital a gas cylinder containing what they thought was laughing gas. However, the cylinder contained not the anaesthetic nitrous oxide but pure nitrogen. When the two men stopped their car to partake of their booty, the nitrogen gas displaced the air in the car, leaving them without oxygen. Had they had any indication of the problem, they could have saved their lives simply by opening the car doors.

These deaths were similar in cause to a relatively common drowning accident known as shallow-water blackout, mentioned specifically in certification classes for recreational scuba diving. When a person is skin diving (that is, without scuba gear), his bottom time is limited by how long he can hold his breath. Occasionally, a skin diver will attempt to lengthen the time he can stay under by hyperventilating before a dive. Unfortunately, this can lead to his losing consciousness underwater, sometimes only a few feet before reaching the surface.

The connection between nitrogen asphyxiation and shallow-water blackout lies in human respiratory physiology. When you hold your breath, you begin to develop a powerful urge to breathe. This is caused not by the depletion of oxygen from your body, but by the buildup of carbon dioxide in your bloodstream, which changes the pH of the blood. The ambitious skin diver "blows off" most of the carbon dioxide in his bloodstream when he hyperventilates; as a result, he notices the urge to breathe much later than he normally would, at a point when his blood oxygen is dangerously low. If his blood oxygen falls too low before he reaches the surface, he blacks out and drowns. Because the Kennedy Space Center workers continued to exhale carbon dioxide with each breath, neither of them noticed an unusual urge to breathe, even though they were completely deprived of oxygen.

## A Humane Execution

Nitrogen asphyxiation is a unique way to die. The victim is not racked by a choking sensation or a burning urge to breathe, because as far as his body knows, he is breathing normally. Carbon dioxide is not building up in his bloodstream, so he never realizes that anything is wrong, nor does he experience any discomfort; he simply passes out when his blood oxygen falls too low.

Nitrogen asphyxiation is therefore a perfect method of execution. It uses a cheap and universally available working medium that requires no special environmental precautions for its storage and disposal. Its first symptom is loss of conscious sensation, a primary goal in a humane execution. It involves no physical trauma, no toxic drugs; the executed man's organs will even be suitable for donation, a factor cited in a 1995 stay of execution for a Georgia killer.

Assuming that the prisoner's guilt has been sufficiently proved, nitrogen asphyxiation is perhaps the most gentle way to deal with him. A condemned man awaiting death by nitrogen asphyxiation would experience no more pain or suffering than he created in his own mind.

# Periodical Bibliography

The following articles have been selected to supplement the diverse views presented in this chapter. Addresses are provided for periodicals not indexed in the *Readers' Guide to Periodical Literature*, the *Alternative Press Index*, or the *Social Sciences Index*.

| | |
|---|---|
| Paul Baumann | "An Editorial Dissent," *Commonweal*, May 19, 1995. |
| Susan Blaustein | "Witness to Another Execution," *Harper's*, May 1994. |
| Sidney Callahan | "The Thirst for Revenge," *Commonweal*, June 16, 1995. |
| Kevin Clarke | "Waiting for Gacy," *U.S. Catholic*, November 1994. |
| Kevin A. Codd | "The Hanging of Westley Allan Dodd," *America*, January 30, 1993. |
| *Commonweal* | "To Kill, or Not to Kill," May 19, 1995. |
| Robert F. Drinan | "U.S. Catholics and the Death Penalty," *America*, September 30, 1995. |
| Terry Eastland | "Blackmun: Still Growing," *American Spectator*, April/May 1994. |
| Randy Frame | "A Matter of Life and Death," *Christianity Today*, August 14, 1995. |
| Cornelius F. Murphy | "The Supreme Court and Capital Punishment: A New Hands-Off Approach," *USA Today*, March 1993. |
| *National Review* | "Quo Vadis?" May 1, 1995. |
| Judy Pennington | "Helen Prejean," *Progressive*, January 1996. |
| Julia Reed | "Witness at the Execution," *Vogue*, June 1993. |
| David Seideman | "A Twist Before Dying," *Time*, May 23, 1994. |
| Andrew L. Shapiro | "End of the Rope?" *Nation*, June 6, 1994. |
| Ivan Solotaroff | "The Last Face You'll Ever See," *Esquire*, August 1995. |
| David O. Stewart | "Dealing with Death," *ABA Journal*, November 1994. Available from 750 N. Lake Shore Dr., Chicago, IL 60611. |
| Morris L. Thigpen | "Managing Death Row: A Tough Assignment," *Corrections Today*, July 1993. Available from 4380 Forbes Blvd., Lanham, MD 20706-4322. |

# Is the Death Penalty an Effective Punishment?

# Chapter Preface

In April 1995, the editors of the *Economist*, a weekly British newsmagazine, remarked that "the heart of the death penalty debate is no longer morality but efficiency. Or rather, inefficiency." Although the death row population in the United States has risen above 3,000, only 300 or so prisoners have actually been executed since 1976, the editors pointed out. The main cause of such inefficiency, they maintained, is the appeals process—the judicial review of trials, guaranteed by the writ of habeas corpus, that ensures that convictions and sentences meet constitutional standards of fairness and justice. Capital trials are automatically reviewed by state supreme courts, and this review is usually appealed to the U.S. Supreme Court. From that point, prisoners may appeal their conviction or sentence first to a federal district judge, then to the district Circuit Court of Appeals, and then once again to the Supreme Court—any of which can overturn the conviction or sentence or send the case back to a lower court for further review.

Anti–death penalty activists maintain that the lengthy process of appeals is necessary to prevent wrongful executions. They contend that criminal trials are often marred by the abuses of prosecutors, the incompetence of defense attorneys, the ignorance of juries, or the harshness of judges. Review by higher courts is essential to ensure that death sentences have been imposed lawfully, they argue. Sam Howe Verhovek, a *New York Times* reporter, reports that "studies have suggested that nearly half of Federal petitions filed in death penalty cases result in either a reversal of the sentence or an overturned conviction." To opponents of the death penalty, this statistic suggests that federal review of capital cases prevents innocent people from being executed.

Supporters of capital punishment contend that prisoners and anti–death penalty lawyers abuse the system in order to delay justice. Once a conviction and sentence have been reviewed by a state supreme court, they argue, there is little need for further review. Conservative columnist William A. Rusher contends that prisoners and their lawyers use the appeals process to look for a sympathetic judge "who will issue as many stays of execution as necessary, on the basis of 'new' contentions however flimsy, to . . . launch a whole new round of hearings and appeals." Rusher concludes, "The wonder is that anybody, however guilty, ever gets executed at all."

Among the viewpoints in the following chapter, authors debate whether the appeals process is too lengthy and expensive to make the death penalty an effective punishment.

*"Only a tiny fraction of even the most vicious killers ever get executed. Neither deterrence nor justice can possibly be achieved in this way."*

# The Death Penalty Is a Deterrent

Thomas Sowell and John J. DiIulio Jr.

In Part I of the following two-part viewpoint, Thomas Sowell maintains that studies prove capital punishment is an effective deterrent to murder. Furthermore, he argues that alternatives to death sentences allow the possibility that murderers will commit further crimes. In Part II, John J. DiIulio Jr. contends that the death penalty would be an effective deterrent if capital punishment were used consistently and if the process had fewer delays. Sowell is a syndicated columnist and a senior fellow at the Hoover Institution in Palo Alto, California. DiIulio is a professor of politics at Princeton University and is director of the Brookings Institution Center for Public Management.

As you read, consider the following questions:

1. According to Sowell, why should high statistical correlations between capital punishment and reduced murder rates not be expected?
2. How many serious violent offenses were committed by commuted prisoners in Texas, according to DiIulio?
3. In DiIulio's opinion, what is the real bottleneck in executing convicted killers?

Thomas Sowell, "Defenders of Murderers Spring into Action," *Manchester Union-Leader*, December 13, 1994. Reprinted by permission of Thomas Sowell and Creators Syndicate. John J. DiIulio Jr., "Retrieve the Death Penalty from Symbolism," *American Enterprise*, May/June 1995. Reprinted by permission of the American Enterprise Institute.

The defenders of murderers have sprung into action. A 1994 feature story in the *New York Times* was headed: "The Rage to Kill Those Who Kill."

The title was a gem. It explained away others' beliefs as mere emotion—"rage"—and created a false moral equivalence. According to the deep thinkers, executing murderers is "repeating the acts that society condemns." Physical equivalence becomes moral equivalence.

If we took this kind of "reasoning" seriously, it would be wrong to take back by force what a robber has seized by force. It would be wrong to imprison someone who had illegally imprisoned someone else. It would be wrong for the police to drive above the speed limit to pursue someone who was speeding.

No ordinary person with common sense confuses physical equivalence with moral equivalence. Only deep thinkers on a crusade do that.

## Studies Show That Executions Deter

The grand dogma of the opponents of the death penalty is that executions do not deter murder. A 1959 study on which this dogma was based was so crude that it was laughable. But it told the anointed what they wanted to hear.

A more sophisticated study, by Professor Isaac Ehrlich of the University of Chicago, indicated that eight murders were deterred by every execution. The anointed jumped all over him, making all sorts of objections to his statistical methods that they never made against the study that supported their prejudices.

One of the problems with statistical studies on this subject is that the era when executions were common and murder rates were low was also an era of sloppy statistics, with all sorts of "homicides"—including fatal automobile accidents—sometimes being included.

Since the death penalty has applied to premeditated murder, it was never intended to deter automobile accidents. And now that the statistics are better kept, executions are so rare and so long delayed that high statistical correlations are not to be expected.

But we do not require high statistical correlations for most policies on most issues. Moreover, we know that the death penalty definitely deters those who are executed. The fact that this is obvious does not make it any less important.

It is certainly not less important to the families of people murdered by those who have murdered before and who have been turned loose by judges or parole boards, or allowed weekend furloughs by "progressive" prison authorities. Whether these additional murders meet the statisticians' technical definitions of "significance," they are very significant to widows, orphans and the parents of murdered children.

"Life in prison without the possibility of parole" is the grand alternative to execution presented by those who consider words equivalent to reality. But there is nothing to prevent people under such a sentence from being paroled under later laws or later court ruling. Moreover, there is nothing to stop them from escaping or from killing again while in prison.

The Supreme Court got us into this legal mess by pretending to find a prohibition or restriction against capital punishment implicit in the Constitution, rather than in the fashionable writings of the anointed. While the 8th Amendment forbids "cruel and unusual punishment," the 5th Amendment—passed at the same time—accepted the legality of the death penalty by saying that it must take place through "due process of law."

---

## The Death Penalty Is a Deterrent

Some politicians—former New York Governor Mario Cuomo always comes to mind—repeat the litany that there is no evidence for the deterrent effect of capital punishment. That falsehood betrays either ignorance or deception. It is indeed ineffective to simply *enact* a death penalty, as is confirmed by the studies that Cuomo likes to cite. But *enforcing* a death penalty is an entirely different matter. For thirty years the economics journals have been publishing evidence for large deterrent effects when death penalties are enforced.

Steven E. Landsburg, *Forbes*, November 21, 1994.

---

This twisting and straining of the law by judges reflects the same influences as the twisting and straining of logic by others among the anointed who confuse squeamishness with higher morality. More fundamentally, however, the death penalty is another in a long series of issues which provide occasions for moral preening and presumptions of deeper wisdom which lie at the heart of the vision of the anointed—whether the issue is crime, foreign policy, or health care.

Most of those who oppose capital punishment tend to oppose punishment in general and to favor "rehabilitation," getting at the "root causes" of crime and other notions that have failed disastrously and repeatedly.

Unfortunately, others pay the price of this bitter end resistance to reality.

# II

Between 1977 and 1993 a third of a million Americans were murdered. Now take this multiple-choice test and guess what happened to their killers:

1. How many people were on death row in 1993 for all those lives stolen since 1977?
   (a)  58,590
   (b)  14,152
   (c)  2,716
2. How many of the thousands of individuals on death row in 1993 were actually put to death that year?
   (a)  491
   (b)  164
   (c)  38
3. Between 1977 and 1993, how many murderers do you suppose were executed in America in total?
   (a)  22,600
   (b)  2,260
   (c)  226
4. What is the average sentence these days of someone in state prison for murder?
   (a)  40 years
   (b)  30 years
   (c)  20 years
5. How much time does the average murderer actually spend in lockup before being released?
   (a)  21 years
   (b)  14.7 years
   (c)  8.5 years

The correct answer to each question is "c." Which means that our justice system's message to anyone who believes murder should be punished by the death penalty in more than just a few symbolic cases is currently something like: "Get lost!"

## When Violent Criminals Are Not Executed

In recent years, no state has executed more murderers than Texas. In 1993 Texas carried out seventeen capital punishments; Virginia was a distant second with five. But Texas, like other states, commuted all death sentences to life imprisonment after the Supreme Court banished the death penalty in 1972, and a recent study tells us what happened to those death row inmates when Texas stopped executing them. It reveals that since 1974 about three times as many Texas prisoners have been released from death row by commutation or judicial reversals or dismissals as have been executed. After being released into the general prison population, 12 of 47 commuted prisoners were responsible for 21 serious violent offenses against other inmates and prison staff. One commuted death row inmate killed another prisoner. And within a year of his release on parole another commuted death row prisoner killed a girl.

106

This is not to say that every murderer on death row would murder again if released. But these individuals do tend to be repeat criminals. Over 40 percent of the persons on death row in 1992 were on probation, parole, or pretrial release at the time they murdered. (Ongoing research by myself and others indicates that perhaps a third of all the murders committed in this country over the last few decades were carried out by persons freed under court supervision. Tens of thousands of Americans are dead today simply because these criminals were let free.)

## Bias and the Death Penalty

One of the things that has obstructed and delayed the carrying out of death sentences most is fear that they might be handed out in racially unfair ways. There are scores of studies that test this by weighing racial factors in capital sentencing. And those studies that control for all relevant factors including crucial legal variables (eyewitnesses present, aggravating circumstances) find absolutely no evidence of racial bias in contemporary capital sentencing. Of those persons under sentence of death in 1993, about 58 percent were white. This is actually much higher than the proportion of all murderers who are white. Historically, black homicide rates have never been less than five times white homicide rates, and in many years since the 1950s have been more than ten times higher.

No matter what type of reforms might be adopted to reduce the endless legal appeals that currently block most death sentences from being completed, America is never going to make it easy or inexpensive to execute convicted killers. Besides, the real bottleneck discouraging use of the death penalty today is not at the back end, it's at the front end: prosecutors wary of controversy don't seek the death penalty if they can help it, least of all in racially charged cases. When the Supreme Court terminated the death penalty in 1972, murder cases fell into the plea-bargaining pit along with other violent crimes. When the Court reinstated the death penalty in 1976, prosecutors were not eager to pull it out. Today, the bureaucratic, mass assembly culture of most big-city district attorney's offices favors doing a little deterrence on the cheap, frankly, not a lot of justice at great effort and financial cost.

Every major opinion survey of the last decade shows that large majorities of Americans—whites, blacks, young and old alike—support the execution of murderers. Americans value the death penalty not just for its utility as a crime-reduction tool; they value it as a way of doing justice. But, somehow, getting away with murder remains relatively easy in America. Only a tiny fraction of even the most vicious killers ever get executed. Neither deterrence nor justice can possibly be achieved in this way.

*"We cannot now conclude that by killing one person we deter others from killing."*

# The Death Penalty Is Not a Deterrent

Richard L. Nygaard and *The New Yorker*

Many of those who support the death penalty argue that it deters people from committing murder. In Part I of the following two-part viewpoint, Richard L. Nygaard maintains that the death penalty only deters the convict who is killed. He contends that because imprisonment would deter these criminals as effectively as capital punishment, death sentences are unjustified. In Part II, the editors of the *New Yorker* assert that widespread support for capital punishment is a response to high crime rates. The death penalty does not deter crime, they argue, and public enthusiasm for it would wane over time if capital punishment were abolished. Nygaard is a judge on the U.S. Third Circuit Court of Appeals in Philadelphia. The *New Yorker* is a liberal weekly magazine.

As you read, consider the following questions:

1. What are the three means of criminal punishment listed by Nygaard?
2. According to a 1991 Gallup poll, cited by the *New Yorker*, what reason do most people give for supporting the death penalty?
3. How many murders were committed in 1991, according to the editors of the *New Yorker*?

Richard L. Nygaard, "'Vengeance Is Mine,' Says the Lord," *America*, October 8, 1994. Reprinted by permission of the author. "A Fondness for the Gallows," *New Yorker*, November 30, 1992. Copyright ©1992 by the New Yorker Magazine Inc. All rights reserved.

# I

$P$erry Carris is dead. (This is not his real name.) I doubt, however, that many will mourn him. Indeed, even among those who did not want him to die, most would readily admit that the world is a better place without him. He was a brutal killer and not one with whom anyone would easily sympathize. He and an accomplice entered the home of his friend's elderly uncle and aunt, then killed and robbed them. The uncle was stabbed seventy-nine times, and the aunt, who weighed only seventy pounds, was stabbed sixty-six times. Carris and his friend had killed them with a bayonet.

But, you see, Perry Carris did not just die—we killed him. One night, officers of the prison where he spent his final hours injected him with lethal chemicals, and quietly he met eternity. And there are many more who are in like fashion scheduled to die. Moreover, the new Federal crime bill imposes death as a penalty for fifty more crimes. Can Christians continue any longer to watch in passive silence? Is it not time to think about what society is doing—what we are doing? Carris's act was deliberate and fully planned. So was ours. Carris's motivation was a cruel disregard for life. What was ours? The first killing was clearly sinful, criminal and unjustified. But how about the second?

Punishment is a theme with which each of us must wrestle. The death penalty as the ultimate sanction brings punishment sharply into focus. It is the surrogate for society's frustration with its government's failures to protect the citizenry and maintain order. . . .

## Justifications for Executions Fail

It is important, first, to know why we punish and why we killed Perry Carris. American penology is really quite simple. We have just three means of criminal punishment: probation, incarceration and death. And we rely upon only four justifications: rehabilitation, deterrence, containment and retribution. How does the death penalty serve these ends? When we look at each possible justification, it becomes clear that both society's motivation and the penological justification for the death penalty are simply retribution—we are "getting even."

First, one can easily reject rehabilitation as an aim. If there is one thing the death penalty surely does not do, it does not rehabilitate the person upon whom it is imposed. It simply takes that person's life.

The second purpose, deterrence, is more problematic. Statistics uniformly show that the condemned on death row did not consider the possibility that they might die for their crimes. There may be others, of course, who thought of the consequences and did not kill. This possibility has been little researched, and as yet we simply do not know much about this aspect of deterrence. The incomplete data, however, indicate that of those disposed to kill, none seemed to fear the consequences. Hence, we cannot now conclude that by killing one person we deter others from killing. What we refer to as "general deterrence" does not philosophically justify the death penalty.

There is a second type of deterrence, "specific deterrence," which is directed toward the person we punish. In this instance none could deny that death works perfectly. Indeed, the person executed can never commit another crime. Death is permanent deterrence. The question here is whether death as a penalty is necessary. All current statistics indicate that it is, first of all, more expensive to execute a person than it is to imprison for life. Second, life imprisonment will protect society from further criminal acts by the malefactor. Consequently penological theorists reject both general and specific deterrence as legitimate justifications for the death penalty.

Containment too is philosophically problematic because it punishes one for something as yet not done. We use the crime already committed to project, sometimes without further data, that the criminal will do it again. Then we contain these people to prevent them from repeating. Unquestionably, although killing the offender does, in a grim and final sense, contain and thereby protect society from potential future criminal acts against it, one must ask again—is it necessary? It is not. Penologists recognize that one can be effectively and economically contained in a prison. Hence they also reject containment to justify the death penalty.

## Retribution Does Not Justify Executions

This leaves only retribution. Revenge. The ultimate payback. As a retributory tool, death works wonderfully. The desire for revenge is the dark secret in all of us. It has, I suppose, been so since the beginning of time. It is human nature to resent a hurt, and each of us has a desire to hurt back. Before there was law, the fear of personal reprisal may have been all that kept some from physical attacks and property crimes against others. But with law, cultures sought to limit personal revenge by punishment controlled and meted out in a detached fashion by the sovereign. Indeed, the Mosaic and the Hammurabic Codes, although severe, were the sovereign's attempt to temper and assuage personal vendettas by assuming the responsibility for punishment, thereby repudiating and curtailing personal reprisals.

The ideal citizen is not a feuding Hatfield or McCoy. Revenge between citizens is antithetical to civilized society. It invites a greater retaliation, which in turn invites counter-reprisal, which again invites more revenge. It contributes to a spiraling escalation of violence between society and the criminal culture. By exacting revenge upon criminals, society drops to the social stratum of its dregs. We are then playing on their terms, by their rules; and we cannot win. Leaders know, and have known for centuries, that civilization requires restraint and that open personal revenge is socially destructive, cannot be permitted and, indeed, must be renounced. Official revenge is no better, and the results are no less odious. By using revenge, by catering to the passions of society, government tells its citizens that vengeance is acceptable behavior—it is just that you, the individual, cannot exact it. Hence, when government does not control crime or is not vengeful enough to suit the demands of its citizens, they lust for more. Vengeance is our conditioned response to crime. It is also, after all, the official response to crime.

# II

Capital punishment enjoys overwhelming public support in this country today. It is, increasingly, one of the things that make America unique.

It has been some time now since capital punishment disappeared from most of the world's industrialized democracies. In country after country, the abolition process was remarkably similar. First, the death penalty fell into disuse. Eventually, it was formally outlawed. In every case, final abolition occurred *despite* widespread public opposition. This fondness for the gallows tends to ebb dramatically over time, however. In West Germany, seventy-four per cent of the population favored the death penalty in 1948. It was outlawed there in 1949, and by 1980 support had fallen to twenty-six per cent. Among people who don't grow up with it, capital punishment comes to be seen as a barbaric relic, like slavery or branding. In Western Europe today, it is no longer a political issue at all.

## Public Opinion and the Death Penalty

A generation ago, this country, too, seemed poised on the brink of abolition. Executions had declined inexorably—from a hundred and ninety-nine in 1935 to one in 1967, and none for a decade after that—and in 1972 the United States Supreme Court effectively ruled all existing capital statutes unconstitutional. The popular backlash was intense: thirty-five state legislatures passed new death-penalty laws over the next few years. And the Supreme Court, as the saying goes, blinked. In 1976, the Court essentially reversed its earlier decision, finding that capital punishment was not, in and of itself, cruel and unusual, and therefore did not violate the Eighth Amendment. The basis for the Court's new ruling was, primarily, the public's support for capital punishment. Elected representatives in other developed countries had found the courage to lead public opinion on this tormented, fundamental question, but under our constitutional system it had fallen to the judiciary to deliver the coup de grâce to the death penalty. And the Supreme Court, whose members hold life tenure largely to insulate them from majoritarian passions, had decided not to lead but to follow.

---

### The Death Penalty Does Not Deter

For years and years, the arguments have raged over whether the death penalty is a deterrent. That used to be, frankly, the only argument when I first began debating it. But the truth is now that because the proponents have never been able to make the case of deterrence convincingly, they have moved to a different argument. It is phrased in many ways, but in the end it all comes down to the same impulse. . . .

Things like this: "Whatever the studies show, people . . . believe that the taking of a life justifies the forfeiting of life." Or: "Our people have the right to insist on a penalty that matches the horror of the crime." Or even this: "An eye for an eye, a tooth for a tooth."

Mario Cuomo, *More than Words: The Speeches of Mario Cuomo*, 1993.

---

Thirty-one Americans were put to death in 1992—the highest toll in thirty years. Internationally, we find ourselves, on this issue, in the company of such nations as Iraq, Iran, and China. Politically repressive regimes and capital punishment are natural bedfellows. And if the publicly expressed impatience of Chief Justice William Rehnquist . . . should lead to the elimination of the legal procedures that currently stall most death sentences we could end up in a class all by ourselves. There are twenty-six hundred people on death row in America. That's enough to have an execution every day, week in and week out, year in and year out, for the rest of the century.

If history is any guide, it won't happen. American public feeling about capital punishment has run in long cycles, with each reformist wave breaking up on the rocks of an era of increased violence. In the eighteen-forties, anti-gallows societies inspired abolition of the death penalty in three states, but disappeared after the outbreak of the Mexican War. A second major reform era ended with the First World War. The most recent reform wave, which peaked in the mid-nineteen-sixties, when a majority of Americans actually opposed the death penalty, was halted by the terrible rise in violent crime which began around that time. The crime rate remains high. Even so, there is more reason to believe that we will eventually gather ourselves for another push toward abolition than to assume that we will continue to drift indefinitely in the other direction.

## The Death Penalty and Deterrence

A perverse sign that we may soon be ready to reason on this subject showed up in a 1991 Gallup Poll. It found that, while seventy-five per cent of Americans support the death penalty, only thirteen per cent think that it has any actual deterrent effect on crime. (And, in fact, many studies have failed to prove any such effect.) When those who supported the death penalty were asked to choose their reason, fully half picked "a life for a life." This is an expression of anger and hopelessness, not a basis for public policy. And the shallowness of people's support for capital punishment seems clear from the sharp drop in that support whenever a strong alternative, such as life imprisonment without parole, is offered.

There were twenty-four thousand murders in the United States in 1991. The process by which all those crimes produce a handful of executions, where it is not simply random, is demonstrably discriminatory: if your victim was white, you are anywhere from four to eleven times as likely to be given the death penalty as you are if your victim was black. As criminal justice, the death penalty is almost entirely symbolic.

*"Appeals currently average nine years and last as long as seventeen years, which precludes the death penalty from being an effective deterrent."*

# A Swifter Death Penalty Would Be an Effective Deterrent

Arlen Specter

On average, death row inmates spend nine years appealing their convictions and sentences before being executed. In the following viewpoint, Arlen Specter contends that abuse of the writ of habeas corpus (which allows prisoners to appeal their convictions and sentences for federal judicial review) causes unnecessary delays that diminish the deterrent effect of the death penalty. He maintains that the endless wait for executions to be carried out results in a miscarriage of justice for both crime victims and defendants. Specter is a Republican senator from Pennsylvania.

As you read, consider the following questions:

1. According to Specter, why is the writ of habeas corpus an indispensable safeguard?
2. What limitations on the use of capital punishment does the author say he has voted for?
3. In the author's opinion, what is the cause of significant delays in habeas corpus proceedings?

Arlen Specter, "Congress Must Make Death Sentences Meaningful Again," *Human Events*, July 15, 1994. Reprinted by permission.

The American people want government to do something about violent crime. Unfortunately, it is now almost certain that whatever crime legislation we pass in 1994 will do nothing about one of the most serious aspects of the crime problem: the interminable appeals process that has made the death penalty more a hollow threat than an effective deterrent.

Both the House and Senate versions of the 1994 crime bill abandoned key provisions that would limit appeals in the federal courts by state death-row inmates. These appeals currently average nine years and last as long as seventeen years, which precludes the death penalty from being an effective deterrent. National polls now show fear of crime to be the No. 1 concern of most Americans. One survey conducted right after President Clinton's 1994 State of the Union Address found that 71% of respondents thought more murders should be punishable by the death penalty.

### The Importance of Habeas Corpus

The great writ of habeas corpus has been the procedure used to guarantee defendants in state criminal trials their rights under the U.S. Constitution. It is an indispensable safeguard because of the documented history of state criminal-court abuses like the 1931 Scottsboro case [in which nine black teenagers were accused of raping two white women and sentenced to death. They were later acquitted]. Unfortunately, it has been applied in a crazy-quilt manner with virtually endless appeals that deny justice to victims and defendants alike, making a mockery of the judicial system.

This incredibly complicated legal process must be understood by the public if sufficient pressure is to be put on Congress to correct this egregious problem.

Delays leave inmates, as well as victims, in a difficult state of suspended animation. In a 1989 case, the British government declined to extradite a defendant to Virginia on murder charges until the death penalty was dropped, because the European Court of Human Rights had ruled that confinement in a Virginia prison for six to eight years awaiting execution violated the European Convention on Human Rights.

Similarly, for survivors of murder victims, there is an inability to reach a sense of resolution concerning their loved one's death until the criminal case has been resolved. The families do not understand the complexities of the legal process and experience feelings of isolation, anger and loss of control over the lengthy court proceedings. The unconscionable delays deny justice to all—society, victims and defendants.

Since it upheld the constitutionality of the death penalty in 1976, the U.S. Supreme Court has required more clearly defined death penalty laws. Thirty-seven [thirty-eight as of 1996] state legislatures have responded to the voters' expressions of public outrage by enacting capital punishment statutes that meet the requirements of the Constitution.

## The Death Penalty Is a Deterrent

My twelve years' experience in the Philadelphia District Attorney's Office convinced me that the death penalty is a deterrent to crime. I saw many cases where professional burglars and robbers refused to carry weapons for fear that a killing would occur and they would be charged with murder in the first degree, carrying the death penalty.

One such case involved three hoodlums who planned to rob a Philadelphia pharmacist. Cater, 19, and Rivers, 18, saw that their partner Williams, 20, was carrying a revolver. The two younger men said they would not participate if Williams took the revolver along, so Williams placed the gun in a drawer and slammed it shut.

Right as the three men were leaving the room, Williams sneaked the revolver back into his pocket. In the course of the robbery, pharmacist Jacob Viner was shot to death by Williams. The details of the crime emerged from the confessions of the three defendants and corroborating evidence. All three men were sentenced to the death penalty, because under the law, Cater and Rivers were equally responsible for Williams' act of murder.

Ultimately Williams was executed and the death penalties for Cater and Rivers were changed to life imprisonment because of extenuating circumstances, since they did not know a weapon was being carried by their co-conspirator. There are many, many similar cases, where robbers and burglars avoid carrying weapons for fear a gun or knife will be used in a murder, subjecting them to the death penalty.

The use of the death penalty has gradually been limited by the courts and legislatures to apply only to the most outrageous cases. In 1925, the Pennsylvania Legislature repealed the mandatory death penalty for first-degree murder, leaving it to the discretion of the jury or trial court. More recently, in 1972, the Supreme Court struck down all state and federal death-penalty laws and prohibited capital punishment for all inmates on death row, or future executions, unless thereafter they contained detailed procedures for consideration of aggravating and mitigating circumstances.

Prosecutors customarily refrain from asking for the death penalty in all but the most heinous crimes. I did that when I was a district attorney—personally reviewing the cases where capital punishment was requested.

While the changes required by the Supreme Court help insure

justice to defendants, there is a sense that capital punishment can be retained only if applied in outrageous cases. I agree with advocates who insist on the greatest degree of care in the use of capital punishment and have voted for limitations to exclude the death penalty for the mentally impaired and the very young. However, I oppose those who search for every possible excuse to avoid the death penalty because they oppose it on the grounds of conscientious scruples.

## Time Between Imposition of
## Death Sentence and Execution, 1977–93

| Year of execution | Number executed | Average elapsed time from sentence to execution, by months |
|---|---|---|
| Total | 226 | 94 |
| 1977–83 | 11 | 51 |
| 1984 | 21 | 74 |
| 1985 | 18 | 71 |
| 1986 | 18 | 87 |
| 1987 | 25 | 86 |
| 1988 | 11 | 80 |
| 1989 | 16 | 95 |
| 1990 | 23 | 95 |
| 1991 | 14 | 116 |
| 1992 | 31 | 114 |
| 1993 | 38 | 113 |

*Capital Punishment 1993*, Bureau of Justice Statistics, 1994.

While I understand and respect that moral opposition, our system of government says the people of the thirty-seven states that have capital punishment are entitled to have those sentences carried out where it has been constitutionally imposed. In those jurisdictions, the debate is over until the statutes have been repealed or the Constitution re-interpreted.

### Abuse of the Appeals Process

Many federal habeas corpus appeals demonstrate virtually endless delays, where judges bounce capital cases like tennis balls from one court to another. Here is an example. After being convicted in California for a double murder in 1980, Robert Alton Harris filed ten petitions for habeas corpus review in the state courts, five similar petitions in the federal courts and eleven applications to the Supreme Court of the United States. Many of those applications to invalidate his death penalty overlapped.

The absurdity of these proceedings is illustrated by the series of decisions involving a Philadelphia criminal, Michael Peoples, who was convicted in the state trial court on charges of robbery and setting the victim on fire. Following this legal trail is not easy, but it is illustrative of the farcical procedures. After the Pennsylvania intermediate appellate court affirmed his conviction, the Pennsylvania Supreme Court denied review in a decision that was unclear whether it was based on the merits or the court's procedural discretion that there was no special reason to consider the substantive issues.

Peoples then filed a petition for habeas corpus in the United States District Court that was denied for failure to exhaust state remedies—meaning the state court did not consider all his claims. The case was then appealed to the next higher court level, the Third Circuit Court of Appeals, which reversed the District Court on the ground that the exhaustion rule was satisfied when the state supreme court had the opportunity to correct alleged violations of the prisoner's constitutional rights. Next, the defendant asked the Supreme Court of the United States to review his case.

Even though the Supreme Court was too busy to hear 4,550 cases that year, the Peoples case was one of the 147 petitions it granted. After the nine justices reviewed the briefs, heard oral argument and deliberated, Justice Antonin Scalia wrote an opinion reversing the Court of Appeals for the Third Circuit.

The Third Circuit then undertook the extensive process of briefs and argument before three judges. It issued a complicated opinion concluding that the original petition for a writ of habeas corpus contained both exhausted and unexhausted claims. That ruling sent the case back to the District Court for reconsideration. This is the short version of what happened in those six courts.

## The Need to Speed Up the Process

Had the District Court simply considered the defendant's constitutional claims on the substantive merits in the first instance, all those briefs, arguments and opinions would have been avoided. These complications arise from a federal statute that requires a defendant to exhaust his or her remedies in the state court before coming to the federal court. The original purpose of giving the state a chance to correct any error and to limit the work of the federal courts was sound. In practice, however, that rule has created a hopeless maze, illustrated by thousands of cases like Peoples and Harris.

The elimination of the statutory exhaustion requirement would mean that Congress, which has authority to establish federal court jurisdiction, would direct United States district courts to decide petitions for writs of habeas corpus after direct appeals to the Supreme Court had upheld the death penalty. From my own experience, I have seen state trial court judges sit on such habeas corpus cases for months or years and then dismiss them in the most perfunctory way because the issues had already been decided by the state supreme court in its earlier decision.

Unless there are unusually complicating factors, which have to be detailed in the district court's opinion, I know that such cases can be heard within two weeks, with no more than a week or two being required to write an opinion. Some district courts have sat on such cases for as long as twelve years. A 180-day time limit would require judges to give priority attention to capital cases.

Even in states with the most prisoners on death row, like Florida, Texas or California, each district court judge would only have such a case every twelve, twenty-five and thirty-six months, respectively.

Decisions on appeals to the courts of appeals should be made within 180 days. That is manageable with priority attention to these relatively few capital cases. The authority of Congress to establish such time limits was exercised in the Speedy Trial Act of 1974, which calls for criminal trials to be concluded within ninety days unless delayed by specified causes.

## Eliminating Trivial Procedural Delays

Significant delays on habeas corpus proceedings are caused by successive petitions to district courts, delays in those courts and repetitive appeals to the courts of appeals. Reform should require permission from a panel of three court of appeals' judges before a successive petition may be filed. This approach would preclude numerous, successive federal habeas corpus petitions like the five filed by Robert Harris in the fourteen-year California case. The successive petition would be permitted only if the facts could not have been previously discovered through reasonable diligence, the claim is based on a new rule, or state officials caused the claim not to be raised earlier.

Obviously, federal habeas corpus is a complex and arcane subject. Its difficult and restrictive rules simply delay imposition of the death penalty and render it meaningless as a deterrent. The purposes of tough law enforcement are best served by full hearings, even in retroactive issues, instead of allowing the procedural morass to defeat the substantive benefits of capital punishment. Practical reinstatement of the death penalty by habeas corpus reform is well worth pursuing, so that meaningless procedures do not remain the enemy of substantive justice.

*"No one can seriously suggest that restricting or eliminating habeas review will have a noticeable effect on violent crime."*

# A Swifter Death Penalty Would Not Be an Effective Deterrent

Wendy Kaminer

Many death penalty supporters maintain that capital punishment would be an effective deterrent if it were carried out more swiftly. They advocate reform of habeas corpus appeals to speed up the death penalty process. In the following viewpoint, Wendy Kaminer argues that limiting death sentence appeals will not prevent crime, since inmates appealing their convictions are not free to commit further crimes. However, she contends, such limitations may keep trial errors from being exposed, resulting in the execution of a wrongly convicted defendant. Kaminer is the author of several books, including *It's All the Rage: Crime and Culture*, from which this viewpoint is excerpted.

As you read, consider the following questions:

1. How does Kaminer define a habeas corpus petition? What does she say is the rationale for it?
2. According to the author, what right does the writ of habeas corpus enshrine?
3. What did the Supreme Court decide in the *McCleskey v. Zant* case, according to the author?

From Wendy Kaminer, *It's All the Rage: Crime and Culture*; © 1995 by Wendy Kaminer. Reprinted by permission of Addison-Wesley Publishing Company, Inc.

To many of us, constitutional rights are a bit like tax breaks: we endorse the ones we use. To some people, a low rate on capital gains is just another loophole for the rich; others claim it indirectly benefits the poor, by triggering investment. Someone who expects never to be arrested might regard constitutional guarantees of fair trial as technicalities and, in the long run, prescriptions for disorder. To criminal defendants, they're inalienable rights.

The "technicality" most maligned in the capital punishment debate has been the writ of habeas corpus, which allows for federal appeals of state court convictions. Habeas corpus petitions, blamed for delays in executions, have been the primary focus of efforts to expand or restrict the death penalty. Proponents of capital punishment advocate strictly limiting or eliminating such appeals, to expedite executions. Abolitionists fight to preserve habeas corpus, viewing it as the last defense against capital punishment and an invaluable safeguard of a fair trial process. Habeas corpus reform was a primary point of contention in Congress for about a decade, beginning in the early 1980s, and was widely credited with preventing passage of comprehensive federal crime control legislation during the Bush administration. Opposition to gun control may have been a more important reason for congressional inaction, but the drive to restrict habeas corpus petitions exemplified the demagogic approach to crime control that has retarded federal and state policy for years. The habeas debate also reflects deep divisions about what Americans should value most in their criminal justice system—fairness or efficiency—particularly in the imposition of the death penalty.

### The Misunderstanding of Habeas Corpus

A majority of Americans may oppose maintaining the writ of habeas corpus, that is, they may oppose extensive federal review of capital convictions—but relatively few Americans understand the habeas debate, which has become hopelessly technical and arcane. (Few members of Congress understand habeas corpus either, Republican Senator Arlen Specter remarks.) Few Americans know that a habeas corpus petition is a vehicle for obtaining federal review of a state court conviction, nor do they know the rationale for this review: that federal remedies must be provided for federal rights. It's likely that few Americans understand the federal system and the division of power between the states and the federal government; few realize that the federal courts are the arbiters of the federal Constitution, just as state courts are the arbiters of state constitutions. How much of these matters a majority of Congress understands is impossible to say.

This is not intended as criticism of the American public. It is not even a plea for civic education. (While most students probably know less about civics than they do about sex, at least civic ignorance won't kill them.) There's no particular reason why educated voters should understand the debate over habeas corpus—unless they find themselves wrongly convicted of a crime in state court. Most people are busy and distraught enough trying to manage their lives, hold on to their jobs, and address law enforcement problems closer to home—gun violence and a variety of street crimes. People pay their elected officials to manage the criminal justice system, among other things, and many take on faith what politicians say about how the system does or does not work. (Some take on faith what may be the ravings of their favorite columnist or talk show host.) So, for a great many people, fear of crime is matched by ignorance of the criminal justice system, which is why support for restricting habeas appeals is easy to muster.

## How the Debate Has Been Framed

"Convicted killers who have been duly tried and sentenced to death by state courts are endlessly delaying their executions with federal appeals, based on legal technicalities, at the taxpayer's expense." That's how the debate about habeas corpus has been framed. Voters who don't understand criminal procedure or the role of the federal courts in vindicating federal rights can surely understand what sounds like a common sense appeal for swift and sure punishment.

What if the debate were framed, instead, like this? Every year a small number of people convicted of crimes, perhaps less than 2 percent of all state inmates, appeal the constitutionality of their convictions in federal court. Only a handful of these are death row cases. Most petitions fail (over 95 percent of petitions in noncapital cases), and habeas corpus petitions are not, in general, a burden for the federal courts: in 1988, for example, habeas petitions constituted less than 4 percent of the district courts' total caseload.

No one can seriously suggest that restricting or eliminating habeas review will have a noticeable effect on violent crime. All petitioners are in custody and are not released to roam the streets while their usually unsuccessful petitions are considered. Occasionally, habeas proceedings do result in long delays in executions of convicted murderers. Occasionally, they prevent the execution of innocent people or, at least, of not clearly guilty people who have been wrongfully tried and convicted in state court. The habeas debate is not a debate about crime; it is a debate about justice.

The writ of habeas corpus, the "Great Writ," enshrines a right not to be wrongfully imprisoned. Congress created federal habeas remedies, for wrongful imprisonment by federal authorities, when it created the federal courts, in 1789. Federal habeas review was extended to state prisoners after the Civil War, when the Fourteenth Amendment was adopted.

---

## Death Penalty Cases Take Time

If the death penalty is to be effective and avoid the constitutional injunction against cruel and unusual punishment (if, in other words, pigs had wings), it ought to be administered swiftly. Then the execution could be connected in the public mind to the crime.

But if that is to happen, then all sorts of quibbles about guilt or innocence or, in many cases, the adequacy of legal representation have to be overcome. Since that is not possible, death-penalty cases take forever to resolve.

Richard Cohen, *Washington Post National Weekly Edition*, July 12–18, 1993.

---

The current debate over habeas corpus dates back to the early 1980s, when the Reagan administration began a campaign to eliminate, effectively, federal review of state convictions. The administration proposed denying review in cases in which petitioners' claims had been "fully and fairly adjudicated" by the state courts; given the broad view of what constitutes full and fair adjudication, this would have precluded federal review in practically all cases. A 1991 report by the American Bar Association (ABA) notes that the "full and fair" standard had an ugly history. It was essentially the standard invoked by the Supreme Court in 1915 to deny habeas corpus relief to Leo Frank, a Jewish man convicted of the rape and murder of a young woman in Georgia, in an outburst of anti-Semitism. Frank was lynched shortly after the Court denied his appeal.

Seventy years later, however, the public was more concerned with crime in the streets than crime in the courts, and Republican administrations, along with several conservative Republican senators, continued pressing for the practical elimination of habeas review. The restrictive proposals were not enacted into law, but they were the subject of much congressional debate about crime legislation during the 1980s and the cause of considerable congressional stasis.

## The Supreme Court Restricts Appeals

What Congress declined to do by legislation, however, the Supreme Court did, in part, by judicial review. While the Warren Court approach to state court convictions had been suspicious, evincing concern for defendants' rights, the Rehnquist Court approach has been deferential, evincing concern for state sovereignty. To protect state court convictions from federal review, the Court erected formidable new procedural barriers to habeas corpus appeals, including a virtual ban on successive petitions (repeated petitions from the same prisoner) and limitations on the retroactivity of "new rules" of law enunciated after petitioner's conviction. Both these rules seem reasonable on their face; both are easy to defend in a sound bite and practically impossible to discredit. But both were unnecessary and unfair. The courts have long been wary of second and third petitions and allowed for dismissal of petitions involving new claims that petitioners had deliberately failed to raise previously. What the Rehnquist Court essentially did in a 1991 case, *McCleskey v. Zant*, was hold petitioners strictly liable for failing to present all claims in their first petitions, regardless of whether their failure was deliberate; this made it easier to execute people despite serious constitutional errors in their convictions, because their lawyers made mistakes. The Court's decision regarding the retroactivity of "new rules" was equally harsh, because "new rules" have been defined so broadly as to preclude the federal courts from correcting mistaken state court interpretations of constitutional law. (This correction would constitute a new rule.) As the ABA points out, this decision, *Teague v. Lane*, essentially sacrificed legal consistency to judicial efficiency: the Constitution will confer different rights on people in different states if state courts can mistakenly adjudicate them with impunity.

These are the kind of arcane legal issues that dominate the habeas corpus debate. The political issues are much simpler: if you're for restricting habeas, you're against crime; if you're against restricting habeas, you're for crime, even though, as a practical matter, habeas review has very little to do with violent crime. Like the political debate, the legal debate is mostly ideological. The campaign for procedural restrictions on habeas does not reflect any empirical evidence of abuses in the current system. In fact, an empirical study conducted by Richard Faust, Tina Rubenstein, and Larry Yackle (published in the *Review of Law and Social Change* 1990–91) suggests that alleged abuses of the writ have been considerably exaggerated. Even advocates of restricting habeas are apt to concede that evidence of abuse is anecdotal. "We've been dealing with horror stories of individual cases," former Bush administration official Paul McNulty says, and "that drives the debate more than empirical data."

## Horror Stories

Horror stories from both sides dominate the habeas debate, as they dominate the debate about capital punishment. Parents of murdered children testify before Congress on one side; innocent men who were sentenced to die testify on the other. At a congressional hearing in May 1993, Robert Stearns described the brutal murder of his son and the agonizing nineteen-and-a-half-year period between the murder and the conclusion of the killer's appeal; ten and a half years were taken up by federal appeals. Rubin Carter testified to the nineteen agonizing years he spent in prison on a false murder conviction, before being released in a habeas corpus proceeding by a federal judge who found that his conviction was based on gross prosecutorial misconduct and racial bias. Carter, who spent years appealing his conviction in the New Jersey courts, noted that his long series of appeals was necessitated by the prosecution's illegal "piecemeal" disclosure of evidence, and "every step took years and at every stage I was the one accused of abusing the system and wasting the court's valuable time on 'frivolous' appeals."

What's striking about these horror stories, on both sides, is their apparently minimal effect. People in favor of habeas restrictions rationalize the stories about innocent people condemned to die by labeling them "anomalous." Or they point with pride to the eventual release of a man who spent years on death row; "the system worked," they say. (The system, of course, has relied heavily on the writ of habeas corpus.) People who want to preserve habeas consider prolonged delays in execution a necessary cost of fairness.

> *"What needs to be stopped is the use of* habeas corpus *to simply go judge shopping."*

# Habeas Corpus Is Abused by Convicts

Kent Scheidegger

Habeas corpus proceedings are meant to ensure the right of criminal defendants to a fair trial that meets constitutional standards. In the following viewpoint, Kent Scheidegger contends that convicted criminals are abusing the process in order to delay their executions. He maintains that state courts consistently uphold constitutional standards and fully and fairly adjudicate death penalty cases. In his opinion, it is unnecessary for federal courts to retry these cases. Scheidegger is legal director of the Criminal Justice Legal Foundation in Sacramento, California, a pro–death penalty organization.

As you read, consider the following questions:

1. In Scheidegger's opinion, what is the single most important function of state and local governments?
2. According to the author, what was the ancient legal procedure of habeas corpus used for?
3. Why was the expansion of habeas corpus necessary in 1953, according to the author?

Kent Scheidegger, "Close the *Habeas Corpus* Loophole," *American Enterprise*, May/June 1995. Reprinted by permission of the American Enterprise Institute.

The jury files back in. They have finally decided. The family members of the murder victim wait anxiously. They've endured the horror of the murder. Then the investigation. Then months of pre-trial maneuvering. Then the trial. Then the penalty phase.

At last the verdict is read. The sentence is death. Now, finally, they think, justice will be done.

But they are tragically wrong. To borrow Churchill's phrase, it is not the end, or the beginning of the end; at best, it is only the end of the beginning.

No one disputes that appeals are necessary in criminal cases. To ensure that trials are fair, some must be reviewed carefully by appellate courts. In complex cases, especially capital ones, this process takes time.

What is very much disputed, though, is the need for the next stage of the current system. In other kinds of cases, once a judgment is affirmed on appeal, the matter is permanently settled and cannot be challenged in another court. Only in state criminal cases are final judgments routinely second-guessed in a different, not higher, court. For after state courts have exhaustively reviewed the conviction and found no reversible error, the convict runs to the federal courts and gets a second review of his constitutional arguments. The careful consideration and rejection of his legal claims by the state courts receives no weight at all in this federal proceeding, called *habeas corpus*.

## Habeas Corpus Causes Unnecessary Delays

The case of Kermit Smith illustrates the unnecessary delay and interference with state proceedings this causes. In 1980, Smith kidnapped three college cheerleaders and brutally raped and murdered one of them, nineteen-year-old Whelette Collins. After his trial, state courts reviewed his conviction in three separate proceedings over a period of seven years. Despite this exhaustive investigation, Smith's lawyers delayed his execution another six-and-a-half years by filing a federal *habeas corpus* petition. Fourteen years after Whelette Collins's death, her killer was finally brought to justice. Nearly half the total delay was in the federal courts, and all this happened in a case with no doubt whatever concerning the identity of the killer.

This practice strikes at the heart of federalism. Enforcement of the basic criminal law is the single most important function of state and local governments. Protection of our persons and property from marauding criminals is a primary reason we have governments in the first place. If states are not competent to try and punish criminals for murder, rape, and robbery, we should begin to ask why we have states at all.

Like so many problems of government excess, this one has its origins in a drastic remedy for a dire problem, a remedy that has both overstayed its necessity and overflowed its banks.

The ancient legal procedure of *habeas corpus* was a remedy for people held in custody illegally. Its beneficiaries included political prisoners jailed by the king and suspects improperly denied bail before trial. The law was clear, however, that a person convicted of a felony in a proper court could not use this procedure to delay or review his sentence.

The latter rule was followed in America into the twentieth century. In case after case, such legal giants as Chief Justice John Marshall, Justice Joseph Story, and Justice Oliver Wendell Holmes reiterated that any claim that did not affect the jurisdiction of the trial court could not be considered on *habeas corpus*, even if the claim were based in the Constitution.

---

## Endless Delays

The machinery of capital justice cranks a lot more slowly now. Death row is a growth industry. The rare inmate to die hangs on close to ten years before meeting the executioner. In Florida, triple-killer Gary Alvord is celebrating his 22d year, still hoping, still appealing. Up the interstate, one quarter of Georgia's 109 death-row prisoners have been there since at least 1980. And in Montana, until May 10, 1995, Duncan McKenzie had avoided the lethal needle for twenty years. In fact, he fell just one vote short of gaining his eighth stay of execution. He may have been the coldblooded murderer of a schoolteacher, but he had chutzpah. His last argument in court: two decades on death row was itself "cruel and unusual" punishment, and therefore a violation of his constitutional rights. Never mind that McKenzie's lawyers had asked for the prior stays and had helped to create the judicial black hole he found himself in. A federal court didn't buy the claim and within days McKenzie became the first inmate executed in Montana since FDR's third term.

David A. Kaplan, *Newsweek*, August 7, 1995.

---

In the 1920s, this practice began to change. Criminal procedure was badly in need of reform, especially in state courts. The old cases are replete with coerced confessions, lynch mobs around courthouses, and indigent defendants tried without counsel or with only perfunctory representation. Looming above it all was the age-old problem of racism.

The Supreme Court expanded constitutional protections to correct such abuses. At the same time, it expanded the writ of *habeas corpus* to cover all constitutional claims, not just claims concerning the jurisdiction of the trial court. In 1953, it dropped the bombshell. Ignoring its own past statements to the contrary, it directed the lower federal courts to redecide issues already fully and fairly adjudicated in the state courts.

## Federal Review Is No Longer Needed

In retrospect, it is not difficult to see why such a step was thought necessary in 1953, especially in a case from the South involving racial discrimination in jury selection. Given the magnitude of the problem, deputizing the lower federal courts as mini supreme courts, with full power to review decisions of state supreme courts, may well have been a necessary evil.

Changes in the law and the nation since 1953, however, have made this practice far less necessary and much more evil. America is a vastly different place than it was. Governors do not stand in schoolhouse doors. Presidents do not need to send the Army to enforce court orders. State judges do not declare that the U.S. Constitution is inapplicable. Federal constitutional limits are acknowledged and applied every day in every criminal court in this country.

The use of *habeas corpus* to review state judgments in federal court can be justified in two situations, both exceedingly rare. First, if a defendant has compelling new evidence of actual innocence which the state will not consider, *habeas corpus* can prevent a fundamental miscarriage of justice. Second, if a state court really does defy Supreme Court precedent, so clearly that reasonable judges cannot differ, a corrective mechanism is needed.

What needs to be stopped is the use of *habeas corpus* to simply go judge shopping, running the same marginal arguments past multiple sets of judges until someone agrees with the defendant.

"Habeas corpus has been threatened by a battery of Supreme Court decisions that have systematically narrowed prisoners' access to the federal courts."

# Habeas Corpus Has Been Undermined by the Supreme Court

Susan Blaustein

The Supreme Court under Chief Justice William Rehnquist has narrowed the conditions under which prisoners can appeal their convictions and sentences to federal courts. In the following viewpoint, Susan Blaustein argues that, contrary to most people's fear that criminals are being released on technicalities, possibly innocent prisoners are being executed without their cases' being fully reviewed by federal courts. Blaustein is a journalist in Washington, D.C.

As you read, consider the following questions:

1. What percentage of habeas corpus petitions have resulted in reversals of convictions or new trials, according to the American Bar Association study cited by the author?
2. According to Blaustein, what did the ruling in the case of *Brecht v. Abrahamson* do?
3. What was the "ominous" result of the case of *Herrera v. Collins*, according to the author?

From "Crimes Against Habeas Corpus" by Susan Blaustein, *Nation*, June 20, 1994.
Reprinted with permission from the *Nation* magazine; © The Nation Company, L.P.

In recent years habeas corpus has been threatened by a battery of Supreme Court decisions that have systematically narrowed prisoners' access to the federal courts. The provisions in the 1994 crime bill would have corrected the most egregious of these rulings, thereby restoring the historic balance between states' and individuals' rights in reviewing criminal convictions. Many constitutional scholars and lawyers and some Democratic legislators believe it is the duty of Congress—which first incorporated habeas provisions into Article One of the Constitution in 1789 and has been responsible for its oversight ever since—to make sure that the current Supreme Court does not jeopardize those essential rights habeas corpus was designed to protect.

Although most habeas petitions are filed by ordinary prisoners, the vast majority of these never make it to federal trial. It is the relatively few petitions filed by death-row inmates that are far more complex, expensive and time-consuming to litigate. Because so many capital defendants are assigned incompetent lawyers and are convicted in seriously flawed trials, an astounding 40 percent of habeas corpus petitions have resulted in reversals of convictions or new trials, according to a 1989 study by the American Bar Association. Figures like this one, coupled with tales of horrific crimes perpetrated by repeat offenders, have led many outraged and fearful Americans to believe, erroneously, that convicted murderers are regularly being freed on technicalities.

### The Supreme Court Restricts Habeas Corpus

Eager to streamline the appeals process and to shorten the average eight-year time lag between conviction and execution, since 1989 alone the Supreme Court has issued more than a dozen rulings that have severely limited the number and scope of claims inmates may bring to federal courts. One line of decisions now precludes death-row inmates who have completed their first round of appeals from benefiting from any new Supreme Court ruling. This not only encourages delays by effectively penalizing inmates who diligently pursue their appeals; it also results in a fundamental unfairness in the application of the death penalty. For example, the same 1993 Supreme Court ruling that would render one man's 1994 death sentence unconstitutional would spell no relief for the inmate with identical claims whose conviction became final in 1992. The former might be granted a new trial; the latter, an execution date.

Another landmark opinion, *Brecht v. Abrahamson*, written in 1993 by Chief Justice William Rehnquist, shifted the burden of proof in federal habeas proceedings from the prosecutor to the prisoner, who must now demonstrate that he could never have been found guilty had there not been a constitutional violation at his trial—an almost impossible standard to meet. With this ruling the Court effectively lent its seal of approval to coerced confessions, the failure to inform prisoners of their right to counsel and the suppression of exculpatory evidence by prosecutors or police, so long as additional incriminating evidence exists. In *Herrera v. Collins*, perhaps the most shocking decision issued in 1993, the Chief Justice held that a condemned person whose appeal is based solely upon strong new evidence of his innocence is not entitled to a federal court hearing. The ominous formulation that one might be innocent but nevertheless may be executed because one's trial has been deemed constitutionally correct is the latest Orwellian twist in the Court's recent habeas jurisprudence.

## The Outcome of Habeas Restrictions

The trial of Cornelius Singleton, who was executed in Alabama in November 1992 for killing a nun in a cemetery by smothering her with rocks, was hardly a model of due process. After begging to be taken off the case, the court-appointed lawyer refused to meet with his client, failed to object when the prosecutor struck all blacks from the jury pool and neglected to tell the jury that Singleton was mentally retarded. He then forged Singleton's name on a petition for habeas corpus; he was later disbarred. Singleton would not have been eligible for the death penalty if he had been properly defended; but six Supreme Court justices agreed in 1992 that he should be executed anyway because of a 1991 decision that prohibits federal courts from reviewing more than one habeas corpus petition from each prisoner unless there is serious new evidence of actual innocence. "It was clear to everyone that the guy got screwed," said a conservative clerk. "What allowed all of us to sleep soundly that night was the knowledge that he was basically guilty."

Jeffrey Rosen, *New Republic*, October 4, 1993.

Still another series of cases, originating in a 1977 Rehnquist opinion, have deprived inmates of federal court review when their lawyers have made mistakes. In 1991, for example, Justice Sandra Day O'Connor held that Virginia death-row inmate Roger Coleman would not be allowed to present new evidence of his innocence because his attorney had been a day late in filing Coleman's habeas petition. Coleman was executed. Apparently, in the High Court's view, punctuality takes precedence over possible innocence.

"The public thinks the defendants get off on technicalities," says veteran capital defender David Bruck. "But the truth is, defendants are being *executed* on technicalities, due to the thicket of procedural obstacles in habeas rulings by the Supreme Court."

## Congress Fails to Protect Habeas Corpus

The habeas provisions proffered by the House Judiciary Committee would have eliminated some of those new procedural obstacles and enabled inmates to have their day in federal court without being able to abuse that privilege by repeatedly filing last-minute, specious appeals. Most important, given what both sides acknowledge is the often deplorable quality of defense counsel in capital cases and the extraordinary complexity of habeas litigation, the provisions would have created a mechanism for assigning experienced attorneys both at the trial level and for post-conviction appeals.

But the 103rd Congress, caught up in heated debate over the horrors of violence and the virtues of capital punishment, was keener on eliminating inmates' weight-lifting equipment and federal college education funds than on bolstering prisoners' rights—particularly with state prosecutors jamming members' fax machines with hyperbolic warnings that "to vote for the euphemistically entitled habeas 'reform' . . . is to vote to end the death penalty.". . .

By abandoning habeas corpus to the ravages of the current Supreme Court, both the legislative and executive branches of government have, by default, endorsed the High Court's draconian agenda on habeas reform, thereby weakening the separation of powers. The entire apparatus of the state is now on record that individual rights rank well below the rights of states to preserve their convictions and the call for speed and finality in executing criminal judgments. In such a climate, a person wrongly convicted hasn't got a prayer.

*"The death penalty . . . results in much greater
expenditures than simple life imprisonment."*

# The Death Penalty
# Is Too Expensive

Michael Ross

Opponents of capital punishment contend that the costs of implementing death sentences exceed the costs of life imprisonment for criminals. In the following viewpoint, Michael Ross argues that the extra funds needed to investigate, prosecute, and
appeal capital cases would be better spent on crime reduction
efforts, including additional police officers and more prison
cells. He maintains that the expensiveness of the death penalty
is ruining the cash-starved justice system. Ross, whose 1987
death sentence was overturned on appeal, is awaiting resentencing in Somers Prison, Connecticut.

As you read, consider the following questions:

1. According to Ross, how much more expensive are capital
   trials than noncapital trials in California?
2. What is the estimated cost for New Jersey to implement a
   death penalty statute, according to the author?

Michael Ross, "A Voice from Death Row," *America*, February 11, 1995. Reprinted by
permission of the author.

"Why should I, an honest, hardworking taxpayer, have to pay to support a murderer for the rest of his natural life? Why not execute him and save society the cost of his keep?" Being on death row myself, I have heard this argument many times. I believe that it is time to bring a few facts to light.

The death penalty in this country is not cheap. The U.S. Supreme Court has repeatedly stated that because "death is different," much higher levels of procedural safeguards are required by the Constitution before it can be imposed. What this means in practical terms is a lengthy, complex and extremely expensive process of litigation over a period of years in various state and Federal courts. In contrast, life sentences are much less complex, and often their appeals are not pursued beyond the state supreme court level.

### The Costs of a Capital Trial

To begin with, it should be noted that the added expenses of a capital trial will be incurred whenever the death penalty is sought, regardless of the final outcome. Therefore, the true cost of the death penalty also includes all the added expenses of the trials in which the death penalty is sought but not achieved. And because around 30 percent of all death sentences are overturned by state and Federal appeal courts, the costs will have to be repeated in a single capital case far more often than when the death penalty is not sought. The death penalty consequently results in much greater expenditures than simple life imprisonment.

The added complexity and expense begin well before the trial itself. The crime has to be investigated more thoroughly by both the prosecution, which must prove the existence of the aggravating factors needed to obtain the death sentence, and by the defense, which must be prepared to argue in mitigation of such a sentence. Evidence must be prepared as to the defendant's entire background, including childhood, mental and psychological conditions, family relations, employment history, prior arrests and convictions, medical history and much more. And because most capital defendants are indigent, the cost of preparing this evidence—both for the state to obtain the death penalty and for the defense to avoid it—will almost always be paid by the taxpayer.

Pretrial proceedings in capital cases are numerous and complicated. Because there is a whole body of Eighth Amendment law pertaining specifically to them, lengthier pretrial motions must be heard by the court. The process of jury selection is also more complex and time-consuming because there are enhanced constitutional implications regarding pretrial publicity, racial prejudice and other areas of possible juror bias. In cases in which pretrial publicity has affected potential jurors, the considerable added expense of a change of venue must be incurred. In addition, jurors must be asked a complex series of questions designed to determine whether they are excludable for various reasons, such as unwillingness to impose a death sentence due to moral convictions.

---

## Financial Facts About the Death Penalty

- The most comprehensive study in the country found that the death penalty costs North Carolina $2 million per execution *over* the costs of a non–death penalty murder case with a sentence of imprisonment for life. (Duke University, May 1993) On a national basis, these figures translate to an extra cost of half a billion dollars since 1976 for having the death penalty.

- The death penalty costs California $90 million annually beyond the ordinary costs of the justice system—$78 million of this total is incurred at the trial level. (*Sacramento Bee*, March 28, 1988)

- Florida spent an estimated $57 million on the death penalty from 1973 to 1988 to achieve 18 executions—that is an average of $3.2 million per execution. (*Miami Herald*, July 10, 1988)

- In Texas, a death penalty case costs an average of $2.3 million, about three times the cost of imprisoning someone in a single cell at the highest security level for 40 years. (*Dallas Morning News*, March 8, 1992)

*Truth Seeker*, vol. 121, no. 5, 1994.

---

Other areas of considerable expense include the trial itself, which is divided into two phases—one to determine guilt, the other to determine the sentence. This bifurcated arrangement makes capital trials longer than a typical non-capital trial. Then there is the appeals process, which is constitutionally mandated. Finally, let's not forget the cost of maintaining maximum security on death rows, the clemency hearings and the cost of the execution itself.

### The Costs of Death Compared to Imprisonment

So what does all this come to? You may be surprised. California estimates that capital trials are six times more expensive than other, non-capital, murder trials. Each death penalty case costs at least $1 million to prosecute at both the trial and the appellate levels. Only two executions have been carried out in California since 1967, but it is believed that the cost to taxpayers has exceeded a billion dollars during the past eighteen years of legal and political battles over the death penalty issue itself.

Florida, with its numerous executions, has spent $57.2 million since 1973. By comparison, the cost of keeping an inmate in prison for life, figured at forty years, has been estimated at $500,000. But Florida has spent at least $3.2 million for each prisoner executed.

Georgia taxpayers were expected to pay a minimum of $15.7 million on defense counsel alone for death row prisoners in 1989. The average capital case takes up to 800 hours of lawyer time. The figure of $15.7 million did not include the cost of paying state prosecutors or the higher cost of keeping death row prisoners in prison.

Texas estimates that a single death penalty case entails an average expenditure of $2.3 million, about three times the cost of keeping someone in a single cell at the highest security level for forty years.

It can be argued, therefore, that the use of the death penalty results in an enormous diversion of funds from areas where they could be more effectively used. For example, New Jersey had to lay off more than 500 police officers in 1991. At the same time it was implementing a new death penalty statute that would cost an estimated $16 million per year, more than enough to rehire the same number of officers at a salary of $30,000 per year. In Florida, a 1990 mid-year budget cut of $45 million forced the Department of Corrections to implement the early release of over 3,000 inmates.

In recent years, ten other states have also reported the early release of prisoners because of overcrowding and underfunding. Texas has no choice but to release inmates who, in some cases, have served only 20 percent of their sentences in order to make way for incoming prisoners. They need more prison space but cannot afford the expansion costs. On the other hand, in just one six-year period, Texas spent $183.2 million on the death penalty. Illinois is a bit luckier, for it has built new prisons, but the money to open them is lacking. It does, however, have the money to maintain the country's fourth largest death row.

## The Diversion of Funds from Law Enforcement

A number of judges, prosecutors and other law enforcement officials oppose the death penalty on precisely the ground of cost, believing that the enormous concentration of judicial services on a handful of cases (many of which will ultimately result in life imprisonment) needlessly diverts increasingly scarce resources from other areas of law enforcement. In Sierra County, California, the local government was forced to cut police services in 1988 to pick up the tab for pursuing death penalty prosecutions. The County's District Attorney, James Reichle, complained: "If we didn't have to pay $500,000 a pop for Sacramento's murders, I'd have an investigator and the sheriff would have a couple of extra deputies and we could do some lasting good for Sierra County law enforcement."

Dallas County District Attorney Norman Kinne also expressed his frustration at the high cost of capital punishment prosecutions in Texas: "Though I'm a firm believer in the death penalty, I also understand what the cost is. If you can be satisfied with putting a person in the penitentiary for the rest of his life . . . I think maybe we have to be satisfied with that as opposed to spending $1 million to try and get them executed. . . . I think we could use [the money] better for additional penitentiary space, rehabilitation efforts, drug rehabilitation, education [and] especially devote a lot of attention to juveniles." And the Chief Justice of the North Carolina Supreme Court, James Exum, stated: "I think those of us involved in prosecuting these [death penalty] cases have this uneasy notion that . . . these cases are very time-consuming and very troublesome and take a lot of resources that might be better spent on other kinds of crimes. . . ."

## Capital Punishment Is Not a Solution to Crime

Our politicians often leap at the chance that the death penalty gives them to sound tough on crime. But what they are really doing is playing on the feelings of anxiety, frustration and anger that most people feel toward the seemingly uncontrollable plague of crime that our country is currently experiencing. They offer capital punishment as a solution, while at the same time more effective services to the community are being sacrificed. The public should not be fooled by such political rhetoric. There are programs that do work to reduce crime, but the resources to pay for such programs are often being diverted into capital punishment costs. Politicians should be working on genuine solutions to crime prevention and control. And the public needs to realize that being sensible about crime is not the same thing as being soft on crime.

The situation was perhaps best summed up by retired Chief Justice John Dixon of the Louisiana Supreme Court, when he said: "The people have a constitutional right to the death penalty and we'll do our best to make it work rationally. But you can see what it's doing. Capital punishment is destroying the system."

I am currently on Connecticut's death row. Perhaps the people of this state have no objection to paying through the nose for this brand of justice—I readily admit to having no objections to running up the cost. But consider this: I am already behind bars and no longer a threat to society, but every dollar spent to assure my death (or anyone else's for that matter) means a dollar less toward the funding of more police, more prison cells, neighborhood watch programs or toward any of the other programs aimed at reducing crime.

*"[Death penalty opponents] have managed to vastly increase the cost of imposing the death penalty while reducing the rate of executions to a trickle."*

# The Death Penalty Can Be Economically Effective

Alex Kozinski and Sean Gallagher

Opponents of capital punishment maintain that it is too expensive to impose the death penalty and much cheaper to imprison a criminal for life. In the following viewpoint, Alex Kozinski and Sean Gallagher contend that the high costs of carrying out a capital trial and execution are the result of procedural obstacles set up by the Supreme Court to assuage death penalty opponents. They argue that in order to reduce the costs and raise the benefits of maintaining the death penalty, society should reserve capital punishment for cases in which the crime is particularly heinous and guilt is clearly established. Kozinski is a judge on the U.S. Ninth Circuit Court of Appeals. Gallagher is his law clerk.

As you read, consider the following questions:

1. According to Kozinski and Gallagher, about how many people have been sentenced to death since 1972? How many sentences have been carried out?
2. What do the authors estimate is the average extra cost of a death penalty case compared to a noncapital case?
3. According to the authors, what would it take to eliminate the backlog of death row inmates waiting to be executed?

It is a staple of American politics that there is very strong support for the death penalty; in opinion polls, roughly 70 percent consistently favor it. Yet the popular will on this issue has been thwarted.

To be sure, we have many capital trials, convictions and death sentences; we have endless and massively costly appeals; and a few people do get put to death every year. But compared to the number of death sentences, the number of executions is minuscule, and the gap is widening fast.

In 1972, the Supreme Court struck down all existing death penalty statutes and emptied the nation's death rows. Almost immediately states began passing death penalty laws to comply with the Court's reinterpretation of the Eighth Amendment. Since then more than 5,000 men and a handful of women have been given the death sentence; about 2,000 of those sentences have been set aside; fewer than 300 have been carried out.

## The Will of the Majority Thwarted

The reasons are complex, but they boil down to this: The Supreme Court's death penalty case law reflects an uneasy accommodation between the will of the popular majority, who favor capital punishment, and the objections of a much smaller—but ferociously committed—minority, who view it as a barbaric anachronism.

Assuaging death penalty opponents, the Court has devised a number of extraordinary safeguards applicable to capital cases; but responding to complaints that these procedures were used for obstruction and delay, it has also imposed various limitations and exceptions to these safeguards. This pull and tug has resulted in a procedural structure—what Justice Harry A. Blackmun called a "machinery of death"—that is remarkably time-consuming, painfully cumbersome and extremely expensive.

No one knows precisely how large a slice of our productive resources we force-feed to this behemoth, but we can make some educated guesses. To begin with, while 80 to 90 percent of all criminal cases end in plea bargains, capital cases almost always go to trial, and the trials are vastly more complex than their noncapital counterparts. If the defendant is sentenced to death, the case shuttles between the state and Federal courts for years, sometimes decades.

The Robert Alton Harris case, for example, found its way to the California Supreme Court six times; it was reviewed in Federal district court on five occasions and each time it was appealed to the Ninth Circuit. The U.S. Supreme Court reviewed the case once on the merits, though on five other occasions it considered and declined Mr. Harris's request for review. Before Mr. Harris was executed in 1992, his case was reviewed by at least thirty judges and justices on more than twenty occasions over thirteen years.

State and local governments pay for the prosecution as well as for the defense team—which consists of at least two lawyers and a battery of investigators and experts; much of this money is spent even if the defendant eventually gets a lesser sentence. California reportedly spends $90 million a year on the death penalty. Once the case gets into Federal court, the United States starts picking up the defense tab and the sums can be daunting. In one recent case, a Federal district court paid defense lawyers more than $400,000, which didn't include the appeal or petition to the Supreme Court. Our own estimate is that death cases, on the average, cost taxpayers about a million dollars more than their noncapital counterparts. With 3,000 or so inmates on death row, to paraphrase Senator Everett Dirksen, pretty soon you get into real money.

Another significant cost is the burden on the courts. More than a quarter of the opinions published by the California Supreme Court from 1987 to 1993 involved death penalty cases. Since capital appeals are mandatory while appeals in other cases are discretionary, much of this burden is borne by other litigants who must vie for a diminished share of that court's attention. Estimating the judicial resources devoted to a capital case in the Federal courts is difficult, but a fair guess would be ten times those in other cases.

Perhaps the most significant cost of the death penalty is the lack of finality. Death cases raise many more issues, and far more complex issues, than other criminal cases; convictions are attacked with more gusto and reviewed with more vigor in the courts. As a result, fully 40 percent of the death sentences imposed since 1972 have been vacated, sometimes five, ten or fifteen years after trial. One worries about the effect on the families of the victims, who have to endure the possibility—often the reality—of retrials, evidentiary hearings and last-minute stays of execution for years after the crime.

What are we getting in return? Even though we devote vast resources to the task, we come nowhere near executing the number of people we put on death row, and probably never will. We sentence about 250 inmates to death every year but have never executed more than forty. Just to keep up with the number of new death row inmates, states would have to sextuple the pace of executions; to eliminate the backlog, there would have to be one execution a day for the next twenty-six years.

## Support for Capital Punishment Remains Firm

This reality moots much of the traditional debate about the death penalty. Death penalty opponents have certainly not won the popular battle: despite relentless assaults, the public remains firmly committed to capital punishment. Nor have opponents won the moral battle: most of us continue to believe that those who show utter contempt for human life by committing remorseless, premeditated murder justly forfeit the right to their own life.

Other arguments against the death penalty also fall flat. For example, the fear that an innocent person may be convicted also applies to noncapital cases; no one, after all, can give back the twenty years someone wrongfully spends behind bars. Our system is therefore heavily geared to give the criminal defendant the benefit of the doubt. Wrongfully convicted defendants are rare; wrongfully convicted capital defendants are even rarer. The case where the innocent defendant is saved from the electric chair because the one-armed man shows up and confesses happens only in the movies.

George Danby, for the *Bangor Daily News*. Reprinted with permission.

Death penalty opponents are winning the war nevertheless. Unable to stop the majority altogether, they have managed to vastly increase the cost of imposing the death penalty while reducing the rate of executions to a trickle. This trend is not likely to be reversed. Even if we were willing to double or triple the resources we devote to the death penalty, even if we could put all other civil and criminal cases handled by the state and Federal courts on the back burner, it would be to no avail.

The great stumbling block is the lawyers: the jurisprudence of death is so complex, so esoteric, so harrowing, this is the one area where there aren't nearly enough lawyers willing and able to handle all the current cases. In California, for example, almost half the pending death penalty appeals—more than 100—are on hold because the state can't find lawyers to handle them.

We are thus left in a peculiar limbo: we have constructed a machine that is extremely expensive, chokes our legal institutions, visits repeated trauma on victims' families, and ultimately produces nothing like the benefits we would expect from an effective system of capital punishment. This is surely the worst of all worlds.

## A Political Solution

Only two solutions suggest themselves, one judicial and the other political. The judicial solution would require a wholesale repudiation of the Supreme Court's death penalty jurisprudence. This is unlikely to happen. Over the last quarter-century, the Court has developed a substantial body of case law, consisting of some four score opinions, premised on the proposition that death *is* different and we must exercise extraordinary caution before taking human life. As we learned a few years back in the area of abortion, conservative justices are reluctant to reverse such major constitutional judgments.

A political solution may be no easier to achieve, but it's all we have left. The key to any such solution lies with the majority, precisely those among us who consistently strive for imposition of the death penalty for an ever-widening circle of crimes.

The majority must come to understand that this is a self-defeating tactic. Increasing the number of crimes punishable by death, widening the circumstances under which death may be imposed, obtaining more guilty verdicts and expanding death row populations will do nothing to insure that the very worst members of our society are put to death. The majority must accept that we may be willing and able to carry out thirty, forty, maybe fifty executions a year but that we cannot—will not—carry out one a day, every day, for the foreseeable future.

## Deciding Where to Spend Limited Resources

Once that reality is accepted, a difficult but essential next step is to identify where we want to spend our death penalty resources. Instead of adopting a very expansive list of crimes for which the death penalty is an option, state legislatures should draft narrow statutes that reserve the death penalty for only the

143

most heinous criminals. Everyone on death row is very bad, but even within that depraved group, it's possible to make moral judgments about how deeply someone has stepped down the rungs of Hell. Hitler was worse than Eichmann, though both were unspeakably evil by any standard; John Wayne Gacy, with two dozen or so brutal deaths on his conscience, must be considered worse than John Spenkelink, who killed only once.

Differentiating among depraved killers would force us to do some painful soul-searching about the nature of human evil, but it would have three significant advantages. First, it would mean that in a world of limited resources and in the face of a determined opposition, we will sentence to death only those we intend to execute. Second, it would insure that those who suffer the death penalty are the worst of the very bad—mass murderers, hired killers, airplane bombers, for example. This must be better than loading our death rows with many more than we can possibly execute, and then picking those who will die essentially at random.

Third, a political solution would put the process of accommodating divergent viewpoints back into the political arena, where it belongs. This would mean that the people, through their elected representatives, would reassert meaningful control over the process, rather than letting the courts and chance perform the accommodation on an ad hoc, irrational basis.

It will take a heroic act of will for the majority to initiate a political compromise on this emotionally charged issue. But as with democracy itself, the alternatives are much worse.

# Periodical Bibliography

The following articles have been selected to supplement the diverse views presented in this chapter. Addresses are provided for periodicals not indexed in the *Readers' Guide to Periodical Literature*, the *Alternative Press Index*, or the *Social Sciences Index*.

| | |
|---|---|
| Scott Burgins | "Jurors Ignore, Misunderstand Instructions," *ABA Journal*, May 1995. Available from 750 N. Lake Shore Dr., Chicago, IL 60611. |
| David Cole | "Courting Capital Punishment," *Nation*, February 26, 1996. |
| *Commonweal* | "What's the Rush?" June 5, 1992. |
| Ruth Conniff | "Life or Death in Wisconsin," *Progressive*, May 1995. |
| S.C. Gwynne | "Guilty, Innocent, Guilty," *Time*, January 16, 1995. |
| Thomas Harvey Holt | "Death Penalty Poster Boy," *National Review*, June 22, 1992. |
| Wendy Kaminer | "Let Them Die," *Redbook*, July 1994. |
| David A. Kaplan | "Anger and Ambivalence," *Newsweek*, August 7, 1995. |
| David A. Kaplan | "Catch-22 at the High Court," *Newsweek*, April 11, 1994. |
| Michael Korengold | "Is There a Lawyer in the House?" *Utne Reader*, November/December 1992. |
| Debra Cassens Moss | "Death, Habeas, and Good Lawyers: Balancing Fairness and Finality," *ABA Journal*, December 1992. |
| Jeffrey Rosen | "Bad Noose," *New Republic*, October 4, 1993. |
| Bruce Shapiro | "Not for Burning," *Nation*, July 17–24, 1995. |
| John Tucker | "Dead End," *New Republic*, May 4, 1992. |
| Sam Howe Verhovek | "Across the U.S., Executions Are Neither Swift nor Cheap," *New York Times*, February 22, 1995. |
| Rebecca Westerfield | "The Death Penalty: Impending Challenges," *Human Rights*, Winter 1995. Available from 750 N. Lake Shore Dr., Chicago, IL 60611. |
| Katherine van Wormer | "Those Who Seek Execution: Capital Punishment as a Form of Suicide," *USA Today*, March 1995. |

# 4 CHAPTER

# Is the Death Penalty Applied Unfairly?

# Chapter Preface

The Supreme Court's 1972 decision in the case of *Furman v. Georgia*, which effectively struck down all state and federal capital punishment laws existing at that time, established the principle that the death penalty must be applied fairly and consistently or not at all. Newly written state laws that outlined trial procedures for ensuring fairness and consistency revived capital punishment in 1976. But opponents of the death penalty charge that it continues to be applied unfairly.

Figures published by the NAACP Legal Defense and Education Fund—which opposes capital punishment and works to end discrimination in the justice system—show that between 1976 and 1996, 122 (39 percent) of the 314 people executed were black whereas 173 (55 percent) were white. Of their 421 victims, 82 percent were white and 13 percent were black. Critics assert that these statistics show that the death penalty is imposed for the murder of a white person far more often than for the murder of a black person, especially when the murderer is black. Despite the Supreme Court's mandate of fairness and consistency, they contend, discrimination still exists in the way death sentences are applied. Noting the inequality, Alabama attorney Kathryn V. Stanley, who represents death row inmates, argues, "If racism is the determining factor in who lives or dies in this country, then *no one* should die."

Other researchers maintain that discrepancies in the application of death sentences for blacks and whites result not from racism but from differences in the crime rates among the two groups. Patrick Langan, senior statistician at the U.S. Department of Justice, has conducted many studies on the relationship between race and arrest and sentencing. He concludes, "I don't find evidence that the justice system is treating blacks and whites differently." Stephen Klein, a researcher at the Rand Corporation, asserts that it is not race but aggravating factors in a crime—such as murder committed during a robbery or rape—that determine whether death sentences are imposed. When the circumstances of crimes are taken into account, he argues, it becomes clear that the death penalty is imposed in a consistent manner for both whites and blacks.

Since the 1972 Supreme Court decision, supporters and detractors of capital punishment have disputed a number of statistical disparities in the application of the death penalty. The viewpoints in the following chapter explore the question of whether death sentences are handed out fairly.

"*Race* is *an important factor in determining who will be sentenced to die.*"

# The Death Penalty Is Applied Unfairly to Blacks

Michael Ross

Many scholars note that a disproportionate number of prisoners and death row inmates are blacks and other minorities. In the following viewpoint, Michael Ross presents statistics showing that blacks are more likely to receive death sentences for capital crimes than are whites, particularly when the victim is white. He argues that this disparity occurs because prosecutors are more likely, for a number of reasons, to seek the death penalty for blacks or minorities who murder whites. The death penalty is unfair when race is the determining factor of who lives and who dies, Ross concludes. Ross, whose 1987 death sentence was overturned on appeal, is awaiting resentencing in Somers Prison, Connecticut.

As you read, consider the following questions:

1. What percentage of those sentenced to die are minorities, according to Ross?
2. What percentage of capital murder victims were white, in the author's statistics?
3. According to the study cited by the author, what are the two most significant points affecting the likelihood of a death sentence?

Michael Ross, "Is the Death Penalty Racist?" *Human Rights*, Summer 1994; ©1994 by the American Bar Association. Reprinted by permission.

> *[The] evidence shows that there is a better than even chance in Georgia that race will influence the decision to impose the death penalty: a majority of defendants in white-victim crimes would not have been sentenced to die if their victims had been black.*

Surprisingly, those words were written by former U.S. Supreme Court Justice William Brennan in 1987 when he criticized the majority of the Court for continuing to uphold a "capital-sentencing system in which race more likely than not plays a role."

Racism is a nasty word and many people would prefer to look the other way and deny its existence. But not only does it exist, it exists in one of the most sensitive areas of our judicial system: capital punishment.

The question of racial discrimination in capital sentencing procedures has prompted an ongoing debate. And racism was a major factor in U.S. Supreme Court Justice Harry Blackmun's 1994 announcement that he could no longer support our country's use of the death penalty.

"I feel morally and intellectually obligated simply to concede that the death penalty experiment has failed," he said. "It surely is beyond dispute that if the death penalty cannot be administered consistently and rationally, it may not be administered at all."

### Racial Disparities on Death Row

There is much evidence to show that race *is* an important factor in determining who will be sentenced to die and who will receive a lesser punishment for the same crime. Extensive research on capital sentencing patterns over the past twenty years has repeatedly found that race considerations, whether conscious or subconscious, permeate decisions of life and death in the state courts.

As of January 1994, according to the NAACP's Legal Defense and Education Fund's publication *Death Row, U.S.A.*, 40 percent, or 1,117, of the prisoners under sentence of death in America were black, despite the fact that blacks comprise only about 12 percent of the national population. In some states, blacks outnumber whites on death row.

Minorities, considered as a group, comprise 50 percent of those sentenced to die.

The following state statistics are from *Death Row, U.S.A.*:

- In Alabama, 43 percent of their 117 death row inmates are black, yet blacks make up only 26 percent of the state's population.
- In Louisiana, 68 percent of 41 death row inmates are black, yet blacks comprise 25 percent of the state's population.
- In Mississippi, 58 percent of their 52 death row inmates are black, yet blacks make up only 36 percent of the state's population.

- In North Carolina, 38 percent of their 128 death row inmates are black, yet blacks make up only 23 percent of the state's population.
- In South Carolina, 42 percent of their 50 death row inmates are black, yet blacks make up only 30 percent of the state's population.
- In Virginia, 50 percent of their 47 death row inmates are blacks, yet blacks make up only 19 percent of the state's population.

And the imbalance is not limited to the South:

- In Illinois, 60 percent of their 162 death row inmates are black, yet blacks make up only 15 percent of the state's population.
- In Maryland, 80 percent of their 14 death row inmates are black, yet blacks make up only 25 percent of the state's population.
- In New Jersey, 56 percent of their nine death row inmates are black, yet blacks make up only 15 percent of the state's population.
- In Ohio, 47 percent of their 127 death row inmates are black, yet blacks make up only 10 percent of the state's population.
- In Pennsylvania, 60 percent of their 168 death row inmates are black, yet blacks make up only 10 percent of the state's population.

And in the two states with the country's largest death row populations—California with 380 death row inmates and Texas with 363 death row inmates—56 percent of that population is non-white.

## The Significance of the Victim's Race

Statistics on race alone, however, do not necessarily prove bias, given that roughly 50 percent of those arrested for murder are black. Far more significant is the racial disparity revealed by an examination of the race of the murder *victim* in cases where the death penalty is imposed.

The 227 prisoners executed between 1976 (when the death penalty was reinstated) and January 1994 were convicted of killing 302 victims. Of these victims, 255, or 84 percent, were white and only 47 were black or of another minority group. While 86 black or minority prisoners have been executed for murdering white victims, only two white murderers have been executed for the death of a non-white—one for the murder of a black man and one for the murder of an Asian woman.

Numerous studies have been conducted to try to quantify the extent of racial disparities in capital cases. One study done in the late 1970s by William Bowers and Glenn Pierce, both of Northeastern University in Boston, compared statistics on all criminal homicides and death sentences imposed in Florida, Georgia, Texas, and Ohio. Death sentences in these four states accounted for 70 percent of all the death sentences imposed nationally at that time. They found that far more killers of whites than killers of blacks were sentenced to death. They also found that although most killers of whites were white, blacks who killed whites were proportionately more likely to receive the death sentence than any other group.

In Florida and Texas, for example, blacks who killed whites were five and six times, respectively, more likely to be sentenced to death than whites who killed whites. And among black offenders in Florida, those who killed whites were forty times more likely to get the death penalty than those who killed blacks.

No white offender in Florida had ever been sentenced to death for killing a black person up through the period studied. A white man sentenced to death in Florida in 1980 for killing a black woman was the first white person in that state to be sentenced to death for the murder of a sole black person and he has yet to be executed.

### Race and the Prosecutor's Judgment

Several other studies, conducted in a variety of capital punishment states, have arrived at the same conclusion: Killers of whites are far more likely to be sentenced to death than killers of blacks.

An exhaustive study conducted in the early 1980s sought to discover why killers of white victims in Georgia had received the death penalty approximately eleven times more often than killers of black victims.

The study found that the two most significant points affecting the likelihood of an eventual death sentence were the prosecutor's decisions on whether or not to permit plea bargains and whether or not to seek a death sentence after a murder conviction. Cases in which the victims were black were far more likely to result in pleas to manslaughter or life sentences upon conviction of murder than were cases with white victims. Black defendants in cases where the victim was white were both less likely than others to have their charges reduced and more likely, upon conviction of murder, to receive the death penalty.

It was found that prosecutors had sought the death penalty in only 40 percent of the cases where defendants were convicted of a capital crime; the others received automatic life sentences without a penalty hearing.

But perhaps the most disturbing finding was that although cases with white victims tended to be more aggravated in general, the levels of aggravation in crimes involving black victims had to be substantially higher before prosecutors would seek the death penalty. Thus, the overall disparities in death sentencing were due more to the prosecutor's charging and sentencing recommendations than to any jury sentencing decisions.

Several other studies have also found significant racial disparities in prosecutors' decisions on charges. The Bowers study found that the victim's race had a significant "extra-legal" influence on whether or not a capital charge would be filed. And a study done by Michael Radelet and Glenn Pierce, "Race and Prosecutorial Discretion in Homicide Cases," found a tendency by some prosecutors to "upgrade" cases with white victims and "downgrade" those with black victims.

---

## Racial Disparities in Executions

Throughout our history, race has figured heavily in the death penalty. Before the Civil War, the Slave Codes mandated execution for any black who murdered a white but allowed a mere fine for a white who killed a black. Postwar laws continued to require different sentences based on the race of the victim. Today, long after our laws have been sanitized of such overt discrimination, the death penalty continues to be reserved overwhelmingly for cases where the victim is white. Of the 236 people executed between 1976 and 1994, over 80 percent of the cases involved white victims while nearly 50 percent of the homicide victims each year are nonwhite. Incredibly, only once in the nation's history has a white been executed for killing a black—where the victim was a police officer and the defendant had also killed a white.

Elliot L. Richardson and Nicholas deB. Katzenbach, *Christian Science Monitor*, June 13, 1994.

---

However, these findings and others like them do not necessarily imply that prosecutors deliberately discriminate in their charging and sentencing recommendations. In areas with a white majority population that strongly supports the use of capital punishment, it is speculated that there is inevitably more pressure on prosecutors to seek the death penalty in cases with white victims than in those with black victims or victims from other minorities. Also, in general, there is more community outrage, publicity, and public pressure when the murder victim comes from a middle-class background, which is more likely to apply to whites than blacks.

The issue was well summed up by the authors of a study similar to the Georgia study, Samuel R. Gross and Robert Mauro, when they wrote: "Since death penalty prosecutions require large allocations of scarce prosecutorial resources, prosecutors must choose a small number of cases to receive this expensive treatment. In making these choices they may favor homicides that are visible and disturbing to the community, and these will tend to be white-victim homicides."

## The *McCleskey* Case

In 1987, the U.S. Supreme Court examined the issue of racial discrimination in the death penalty in the case of *McCleskey v. Kemp* to determine if Georgia's capital punishment system violated the equal protection clause of the Fourteenth Amendment. The Court demanded a seemingly impossible level of proof for the defendant, who was required to prove either that the decisionmakers in his particular case had acted with a discriminatory intent or purpose, or that the Georgia state legislature had enacted or maintained the death penalty statute because of an anticipated racially discriminatory effect.

The Court, by a narrow five-to-four majority, concluded that statistics alone do not prove that race entered into any capital sentencing decision in any one particular case. The Court further noted that "Any mode for determining guilt or punishment has its weaknesses and potential for misuse. Despite such imperfections, constitutional guarantees are met when the mode for determining guilt or punishment has been surrounded with safeguards to make it as fair as possible."

However, the majority did indicate that the arguments should be presented to the individual state legislative bodies for it is their responsibility, not the Court's, to determine the appropriate punishment for particular crimes. The justices noted that "Despite McCleskey's wide ranging arguments that basically challenge the validity of capital punishment in our multi-racial society, the only question before us is whether in his case . . . the law of Georgia was properly applied."

In a dissenting opinion, Justice John Paul Stevens noted that "the Court's decision appears to be based on a fear that acceptance of McCleskey's claim would sound the death knell for capital punishment. . . . If society were indeed forced to choose between a racially discriminatory death penalty (one that provides heightened protection against murder 'for whites only') and no death penalty at all, the choice mandated by the Constitution would be plain."

## The Racial Justice Act

Following the McCleskey ruling, a congressional bill entitled the Racial Justice Act was drafted. The bill would forbid "racially disproportionate capital sentencing" and would outlaw death sentences found to have been imposed in a racially discriminatory manner. It was debated and defeated in the U.S. Senate by a vote of 52 to 35 on October 13, 1988.

In subsequent years, this same bill has been consistently defeated on every occasion that it has come up for a vote.

Justice Brennan once wrote, "We have demanded a uniquely high degree of rationality in imposing the death penalty. A capital-sentencing system in which race more likely than not plays a role does not meet this standard."

Race will undoubtedly continue to be a factor in sentencing decisions. However, until we can find a way for our society to solve its problems with racial discrimination in the judicial system, we should not allow race to be a factor in determining who lives and who dies.

*"Racial prejudice is not a significant determinant of execution rates."*

# The Death Penalty Is Not Applied Unfairly to Blacks

Stanley Rothman and Stephen Powers

Many opponents of capital punishment assert that blacks are given death sentences more frequently than are whites due to racism in the system. In the following viewpoint, Stanley Rothman and Stephen Powers argue that black criminals receive a disproportionate share of death sentences, particularly when their victims are white, not because of racism but because of the nature of the crimes they commit. They maintain that black on white murders often include the aggravating circumstances that merit the death penalty, whereas black on black murders usually do not. Rothman is director of the Center for the Study of Social and Political Change at Smith College in Northampton, Massachusetts. Powers is a research assistant at the center.

As you read, consider the following questions:

1. According to analysts cited by Rothman and Powers, what percentage of homicides are intraracial?
2. According to Joseph Katz, cited by the authors, what aggravating factors are more often involved in black on white murders than in black on black crimes?
3. In the authors' opinions, why are the jury system and judicial discretion indispensable to social justice?

From Stanley Rothman and Stephen Powers, "Execution by Quota?" Reprinted from the *Public Interest* 116 Summer 1994, pp. 4–5, 9–14; © 1994, National Affairs, Inc., by permission.

The employment of the death penalty as the ultimate criminal sanction has been the subject of enormous debate. Execution has been challenged not only on moral and religious grounds, but more recently on constitutional grounds—as a violation of the Eighth Amendment's protection against cruel and unusual punishment. Opponents of the death penalty contend that it is employed so arbitrarily as to amount to a game of state-sponsored Russian roulette. While the Supreme Court has not ruled capital punishment to be unconstitutional, in 1972 it held that the death penalty was unconstitutional as then practiced, finding evidence of arbitrariness sufficient to require that states overhaul death sentencing procedures.

One of the most controversial aspects of the arbitrariness claim is the charge—leveled by numerous activists and social scientists—that the death penalty has been applied in a manner unfair to blacks. In *Furman vs. Georgia* (1972), several members of the Court observed that racial discrimination had produced different patterns of sentencing and rates of execution for blacks and whites. Indeed, numerous studies of the late 1800s and early 1900s have found that blacks were executed in disproportionate numbers, particularly when the victims of their crimes were white. . . .

But is death sentencing truly discriminatory? The truth is complicated by a number of factors that opponents of the death penalty have tended to discount or ignore. There appear to be legitimate reasons for racially disparate sentencing. Indeed, a number of social scientists have argued that racial prejudice is not a significant determinant of execution rates. These social scientists have demonstrated that when a number of legal factors are taken into account, the relationship between a defendant's race and the likelihood of execution tends to disappear. Why, we must ask, in spite of the questionable validity of the discrimination thesis, does the death penalty continue to be assailed as one of the most repugnant manifestations of American racism? . . .

## Who Kills Whom and Why

The vast majority of murderers who receive the death penalty are involved in intra-racial offenses—that is, in cases of whites killing whites or blacks killing blacks. Most analysts agree that between 92 and 97 percent of homicides are intra-racial. In the much smaller number of cases in which blacks kill whites, the circumstances surrounding the crimes appear to be substantially different. (The number of cases in which whites kill blacks is usually too small to be factored into analyses.)

Black on black homicides are most likely to occur during altercations between persons who know one another. On the other hand, black on white homicides (and to a somewhat lesser extent, white on white) are often committed during the course of a felony or by a multiple offender. In fact, these are examples of aggravating conditions that the Supreme Court has held to be valid criteria in determining sentence severity. Yet while judges and juries take these factors into account, sociological studies often do not. Lest one think the motivation of judges and juries is racism, these factors are given consideration in societies all over the world, whatever their racial composition. They are seen universally as both fair and conducive to public order.

The key issue, then, is whether blacks convicted of killing whites are more likely to be executed because of the racial identity of their victims or because of qualitative differences in the nature of their crimes. In fact, the latter is clearly the case and would appear to explain much of the racial disparity in death sentencing.

## The McCleskey Case

One of the most effective challenges to the claim of racial discrimination actually arose in a court case that supporters of the discrimination thesis had hoped would prove their point. In the 1980s, the National Association for the Advancement of Colored People (NAACP) funded a major study of the effect of race on criminal sentencing. The study, directed by university professors David Baldus, Charles Pulaski, and C. George Woodworth, gained notoriety when it was used in the defense of Warren McCleskey, a black man sentenced to death for the shooting of a white police officer in Georgia. Defense attorneys relied on the Baldus study to substantiate their claim of systemic discrimination against black defendants. The study showed that in cases of mid-range aggravation, blacks who killed whites were more likely to receive the death penalty than whites who killed whites. (In cases of low and high aggravation, the study found race to be an insignificant factor.) The authors of the study argued that racial bias occurred because prosecutors and juries were prejudiced.

The attorneys prosecuting McCleskey countered by hiring an expert methodologist, Joseph Katz, who analyzed the NAACP study and found a number of conceptual and methodological problems. For one, it turned out that police reports often did not include some of the case circumstances that were supposed to have been weighted in the study. In these instances, the researchers recorded that the circumstances were not present, when, in fact, that was not possible to determine. Katz also pointed out that the researchers frequently weighted aggravating conditions in subjective ways. Most importantly, he argued that the researchers had not accounted satisfactorily for the fact that black offender–white victim homicides were often quite different from intra-racial homicides. Katz showed that black on white murders tended to be the most aggravated of all, and frequently were combined with armed robbery, as McCleskey's was. Katz also testified that by Baldus's own measures, McCleskey's was not a mid-range case but a highly aggravated one, and that in such cases the death penalty was as likely to be applied to whites as blacks.

## The Race of the Victim

The Supreme Court ended up rejecting the McCleskey defense, and ruled that statistical models alone do not provide sufficient evidence of discrimination. Later, Katz testified before the Senate Judiciary Committee, and offered further evidence of the differences between homicides in which blacks kill blacks and blacks kill whites. Katz reported that the reason why 11 percent of blacks who killed whites in Georgia received the death penalty—as opposed to only 1 percent of blacks who killed blacks—was that the killings of whites more often involved armed robbery (67 percent of the black on white cases, compared with only 7 percent of the black on black cases). In addition, black on white murders more frequently involved kidnapping and rape, mutilations, execution-style murders, tortures, and beatings. These are all aggravating circumstances that increase the likelihood of a death sentence.

By contrast, 73 percent of the black victim homicides were precipitated by a dispute or fight, circumstances viewed by the courts as mitigating. Katz also observed that 95 percent of black victim homicides were committed by black offenders, and that there were so few white on black cases that no distinctive homicide pattern could even be ascertained. Among the fewer than thirty Georgia cases identified by Katz as white on black, mitigating circumstances seemed to outweigh aggravating. These crimes rarely involved a contemporaneous felony and often were precipitated by a fight. This pattern may or may not hold outside of Georgia, but as of Summer 1994 there has been no detailed national study of white on black crime. (Research has also shown that death sentences are especially likely in cases in which police officers are killed in the line of duty, and that 85 percent of police officers killed are white.)

## No Evidence of Discrimination

Some findings suggest that blacks may actually be treated more leniently than whites. Analysts at the Bureau of Justice Statistics have pointed out that the percentage of inmates on death row who are black (42 percent) is lower than the percentage of criminals charged with murder or non-negligent manslaughter who are black (48 percent). If the legal system still discriminates against blacks, why do they make up a higher percentage of those charged with murder than those executed for murder?

Some critics reply that the police may be more likely to arrest and charge blacks than whites. Yet we have found few data that support this assertion. In fact, Patrick Langan, a senior statistician at the Bureau of Justice Statistics, investigated the possibility of such discrimination and found little evidence of it. Langan based his research on victims' reports of the race of offenders, and found that blacks were sentenced at rates similar to those one would expect given the reports of victims. Obviously, this kind of research could not be conducted for murder cases (because the victims are dead) but the research suggests that the discriminatory arrest argument is highly problematic.

## Justice by Quota

A twist on the racial-disparity argument says that, even if black murderers are no more likely to be executed than white murderers, black murderers are more likely to get the death penalty when they kill whites than when they kill blacks. But there is a commonsense explanation for this phenomenon that has nothing to do with racism. When a murder involves people of different races, it is more likely that the victim and the killer are strangers, and such murders tend to be of the kinds where the death penalty applies. Whites are significantly more likely to be murdered by a stranger—and by someone of a different race—than blacks are.

J. Daryl Charles, *National Review*, September 12, 1994.

In the federal courts, the discrimination argument has found little support. In a number of cases, judges have concluded that the evidence of systemic bias is extremely weak. Rather than order an overhaul of the legal system on the basis of highly problematic and conflicting social science research, judges have preferred to adjudicate discriminatory sentencing claims on a case by case basis. The preferred corrective has been procedural reforms. A number of states have adopted clearer sentencing standards, various provisions to remove extra-legal influences, and the judicial review of death sentences.

## Ideology Prevails

Why, then, have some researchers continued to find evidence of racial discrimination? One possible explanation is that while the sociologists who design death penalty studies are most interested in and competent to measure such variables as the demographic characteristics of groups, these sociologists are ill-equipped to assess the importance of the legal variables that influence the operation of the criminal justice system. In the past, researchers did not bother to control for even the most obvious of legal variables.

Yet despite the crudeness of their methods, sociologists have concluded confidently that racism in the legal system is rampant. Mindful of the history of racial discrimination in capital cases, sociologists perhaps are predisposed to conclude that discrimination persists today. It seems obvious.

An additional difficulty with many of the sociologists is that their assumptions concerning discrimination are often overly idealistic—for example, the belief that extra-legal variables must be entirely absent from the criminal justice system for it to be legitimate, and the assumption that complete objectivity is even possible. Taken to their logical extremes, these kinds of utopian beliefs would require us to condemn virtually every legal system in the history of the world. At best, legal systems are imperfect institutions, reflecting community standards of fairness and objectivity. The jury system and judicial discretion are indispensable instruments of social justice, which permit broad principles to be tailored to the particulars of each case. Without these instruments, and the attendant margin of error or abuse that all free exercises of judgment hazard, the legal system would be doomed either to excessive punishments or to a forbearance that placed innocent individuals at great risk.

While there is justification for the claim that discriminatory capital sentencing and execution occurred in the past, the charge that they persist today lacks support. The best available evidence indicates that disproportionate numbers of blacks commit murder, and that in those cases in which the victims are white the crimes generally are aggravated. . . .

## Politics and the Death Penalty

Clearly there are reasons other than statistical analysis for the continued belief that the legal system discriminates against black defendants. Those who oppose the death penalty on principle, for example, tend to incorporate the discrimination argument into their litany of protest. These critics perceive capital punishment as a vestige of an outmoded, barbaric, and irrational penal code. Black elites, meanwhile, often perceive discrimination in places others do not. They are joined by members of the white cultural establishment, who are quick to sympathize with those who allege racial unfairness.

This may sound like a harsh indictment, but how else are we to explain the facts? For decades, those who argued that the death penalty was administered in a biased manner maintained that the fact that more blacks were executed than whites revealed a lack of concern for black lives. When this argument became untenable—when it became clear that white murderers were actually more likely to be executed than black murderers—these same critics turned to other, equally unsatisfactory arguments. Now, however, they reject the implication of their previous view—that the execution of a larger percentage of whites than blacks must reveal a lack of concern for white lives. The only issue now is the race of the criminal's victim. These critics rationalize their position, but, we submit, their stance can be explained only by a need to find racism everywhere. One is reminded of the wolf in Aesop's fable. The wolf insisted that the lamb was injuring him, and was quick to change his story each time the lamb pointed out the factual errors in his claims. Finally, the wolf killed and ate the lamb anyway, proving that desire can overcome the failure of rationalization.

If the controversy over racial discrimination and the death penalty turned on the merits of the research, politicians would have to concede that death penalty discrimination has been virtually eliminated. Alas, the news media have done little to clarify matters. Most reporting on the issue is inaccurate. An article that appeared in the *New York Times* on April 21, 1994, is typical. The article concluded as follows:

> That some bias occurs is not much at issue. Many studies show that juries mete out the death penalty to black and other minority defendants in a disproportionate number of murder cases, particularly when the victims are white and especially in states and counties that have a history of racial problems.

In fact, as we have shown, these comments are patently false.

## "It is primarily the poor and underprivileged whom the state is determined to kill."

# The Death Penalty Is Applied Unfairly to the Poor

Nick DiSpoldo

In 1972, in the case of *Furman v. Georgia*, the Supreme Court ruled that the death penalty was unconstitutional if it was applied in an arbitrary or discriminatory manner. In the following viewpoint, Nick DiSpoldo argues that the justice system, and particularly the system of capital punishment, discriminates against the poor. He contends that despite judicially guaranteed rights to effective legal defense counsel and adequate legal resources, indigent prisoners do not get the same quality of defense that wealthy defendants receive. DiSpoldo is a freelance writer in Yermo, California.

As you read, consider the following questions:

1. In DiSpoldo's view, what will a rich defendant do when charged with a capital crime that a poor defendant cannot do?
2. According to the author, what Supreme Court ruling established that defendants in capital trials were entitled to free counsel?
3. What Supreme Court ruling established that prisons must maintain law libraries, according to the author?

Nick DiSpoldo, "Capital Punishment and the Poor," *America*, February 11, 1995. Reprinted by permission of the author.

As an inmate and law clerk in the prisons of California and Nevada, I often assisted death row prisoners with legal problems and have studied more death transcripts than I care to recall. I am often asked why I helped people avoid execution who were convicted of horrible crimes. But I'm a paralegal, not a priest or moral philosopher, and am more concerned with due process and equal protection as guaranteed by the Fourteenth Amendment.

## Unequal Justice

The decision of the Los Angeles County District Attorney not to seek the death penalty in the O.J. Simpson case has renewed debate about how fairly the death penalty is applied. In *Griffin v. Illinois*, the late Justice Hugo L. Black wrote: "There can be no equal justice when the kind of trial a man gets depends on how much money he has in his pocket." It is interesting to note that Mr. Simpson is being tried in the same courthouse in which the State of California tried Caryl Chessman. Chessman, a defendant with "no money in his pocket," was convicted of multiple counts of rape and kidnapping and drew the death penalty in 1949. Chessman did not kill anyone but was convicted under the Little Lindberg Law. [Until the 1968 case of *United States v. Jackson* overturned it, this federal law permitted juries to impose death sentences on kidnappers who harmed their victims.] He was executed on May 2, 1960. A poor defendant without friends or family, Chessman chose to defend himself rather than proceed to trial with a public defender who could not, in his opinion, adequately answer legal questions.

I do not, of course, begrudge Mr. Simpson his financial resources; he earned them. But it is nearly impossible, even upon conviction, to execute any individual of wealth, one who is represented by nine attorneys and no one knows how many investigators who assist them. The newest defense addition is a costly team of juror consultants.

I oppose capital punishment because we do not have the capacity to make capital punishment fair, as the Supreme Court believed it could be made fair in *Furman v. Georgia*. "Capacity" is the operable word here. If two suspects, one wealthy, one poor, are charged with separate capital crimes, the quality of justice immediately changes. The rich defendant may usually post bail, retain attorneys of choice, hire investigators and employ experts who will provide psychiatric testimony for the defense. The trial is often delayed for the benefit of the defense by legal maneuvers and multiple motions. The Simpson defense team moved for a speedy trial in accordance with their client's own wishes. However, they could have delayed this trial had it suited their purposes. By way of contrast, the indigent defendant, unable to post bond, will remain in jail and will proceed to trial with a court-appointed attorney or, as is likely, a public defender who is generally either inexperienced or burdened with a staggering caseload.

In researching a book-in-progress about the 300-year history of the death penalty in the United States I have discovered only six cases in which those executed were individuals of influence or affluence. It is primarily the poor and underprivileged whom the state is determined to kill.

We have a death penalty in this country because the Supreme Court has thus far declared it to be constitutional. The Court may again take up the issue and could conceivably declare the death penalty unconstitutional by a mere five-to-four vote—that is how precarious the political and legal life of capital punishment is. The Court has long wrestled with the question of capital punishment. In the 19th century, it decided that execution by firing squad was not "cruel and unusual punishment" (*Wilkerson v. Utah*). In 1890 William Kemmler, the first person to be executed by electrocution, appealed his case and the Court ruled that "punishments are cruel when they involve torture or a lingering death; but the punishment of death is not cruel within the meaning of the Constitution."

---

### "Rights" and the Poor

Perhaps we can shrug off and shred some of the dangerous myths laid on our minds like a second skin—such as the "right" to a fair and impartial jury of our peers; the "right" to represent oneself; the "right" to a fair trial, even. They're *not* rights—they're privileges of the powerful and rich. For the powerless and the poor, they are chimeras that vanish once one reaches out to claim them as something real or substantial.

Mumia Abu-Jamal, *Live from Death Row*, 1995.

---

However, death by electrocution may very well involve "torture" or "a lingering death." On May 3, 1946, Willie Francis was placed in the electric chair in Louisiana's Angola Prison and given the first official and authorized voltage of electricity. The affidavit of Warden Harold Resweber declares: "The electrocutioner turned on the switch. . . . Francis' lips puffed out and he groaned and jumped so that the chair jumped off the floor. The switch was turned on again and the condemned man yelled, 'Take it off! Let me breathe!'" Francis was re-electrocuted, and this time the state accomplished its macabre mission. It is worth noting that as of October 1994 U.S. District Court Judge Marilyn Hall Patel has declared California's gas chamber to be an in-

164

humane method of execution and has halted any further executions in California by this means.

Lewis E. Lawes, former warden of New York's Sing Sing Prison, wrote in *Life and Death in Sing Sing* (1928): "Not only does capital punishment fail in its justifications, but no punishment could be invented with so many defects. It is an unequal punishment in the way it is applied to the rich and the poor. The defendant of wealth or power never goes to the electric chair or gallows." In a book of his own, *Crime in America* (1970), former Attorney General Ramsey Clark observed: "It is the poor, the sick, the ignorant, the powerless and the hated who are executed. . . ."

## Changing Standards on the Supreme Court

The Supreme Court itself may change from decade to decade to such a marked degree that life-and-death issues like capital punishment become a sort of judicial game. For example, between 1930 and 1968, 455 persons were executed for rape in the United States; 405 blacks, 48 whites, 2 Asians. But in 1977 the Court decided in *Coker v. Georgia* that the death penalty for the rape of an adult female was unconstitutional. Fine. But what do we do about the 455 persons who have already been "constitutionally" executed for the crime of rape? There is an old adage in law: At any given time, the Constitution means what the Supreme Court says it means.

I have found that most people are amazed—if not appalled—to learn that prior to 1932 indigent defendants in capital cases were not provided with state-paid counsel. In other words, before 1932 many were executed without having had a lawyer to defend them. In that year the Court ruled (*Powell v. Alabama*) that in capital cases free counsel must be provided for defendants who could not afford to pay. Later, in the 1963 case *Gideon v. Wainwright*, the Court held that all persons charged with felonies in state trials must be furnished free counsel if necessary.

There is no more stunning and startling example of the Court's judicial ambivalence than the case of Frank Palko. In 1935 Frank Palko was convicted of killing a police officer. A Connecticut jury found Palko guilty of second-degree murder and sentenced him to life in prison. The prosecution, dissatisfied with the sentence, appealed the verdict to the Connecticut Court of Errors, citing errors prejudicial to the prosecution. The prosecution was granted the right to retry Palko. Palko objected, citing the Fifth Amendment's prohibition against double jeopardy. Palko had a point. The Fifth Amendment is unequivocal and clear: ". . . nor shall any person be subject for the same offense to be twice put in jeopardy of life or limb. . . ." Yet Palko was retried and this time he was sentenced to death.

Palko appealed to the Supreme Court, which ruled that the Fifth Amendment did not apply to the states. In 1937, Justice Benjamin Cardozo, writer of the Palko decision, accordingly stated: "The Fifth Amendment is not directed to the states, but solely to the Federal Government." So Frank Palko was executed. Thirty-two years later, however, the Warren Court held: "The double jeopardy clause is fundamental to the American scheme of justice and should apply to the states . . . [and] as it is inconsistent with this holding, *Palko v. Connecticut* is hereby overruled." Frank Palko will certainly be happy to hear that.

### Resources for Indigent Defendants

While a prisoner in the Arizona State prison at Florence, I was the administrative clerk of Warden Harold J. Cardwell. I had the run of the prison, and the warden would let me go anywhere except home. I visited the men on death row nearly every other day, and it was my function as law clerk to bring them law books from the prison library, writing materials, copies of advanced court opinions; to make photocopies and to explain how to use the books or read citations. In *Bounds v. Smith* the Court ordered that all prisons must maintain law libraries or provide inmates with "adequate appeal representation and legal instruction." Prison officials opted for the former as being less costly.

These are the limited resources and opportunities available to the indigent in prison. Providing law books, of course, is not necessarily a panacea. Most condemned inmates are poorly educated. Law books can be very difficult, if not impossible, for people who have not read a single book in their lives—about law or anything else.

The grounds for appeal of most death sentences relate to what is called ineffective assistance of counsel. When the Supreme Court demanded that counsel be provided for indigent defendants in *Gideon*, it stressed that assistance means *effective* assistance of counsel. In examining trial transcripts, I often discovered instances where the defense attorney was ineffective: failure to file a timely motion to suppress evidence; failure to challenge defective warrants; inept questioning of prospective jurors, etc. I have read trial records indicating that the entire jury was seated in three hours! When one considers the large pool of prospective jurors and the seventy-five pages of questions they were required to fill out in the Simpson trial, one can be sure that no indigent defendant will ever receive this sort of lengthy pre-trial preparedness.

Capital punishment is a manifestly unfair form of punishment, and for this reason I am convinced that it will eventually be removed from our justice system. We cannot invest society with a respect for human life by taking human life.

*"If guilty whites or wealthy people escape the gallows and guilty poor people do not, the poor or black do not become less guilty because the others escaped their deserved punishment."*

# The Death Penalty Is Not Unfair to the Guilty

Ernest van den Haag

If a poor defendant is guilty, it does not matter that the death penalty discriminates against the poor, Ernest van den Haag states in the following viewpoint. Van den Haag argues that all murderers, whether rich or poor, deserve to be executed. The death penalty's only injustice is in society's failure to execute some wealthy murderers as well, he contends. Van den Haag is John M. Olin professor emeritus of jurisprudence and public policy at Fordham University in the Bronx, New York, and the author of *Punishing Criminals: Concerning a Very Old and Painful Question.*

As you read, consider the following questions:

1. What symbolic and moral importance does the death penalty have, in the author's opinion?
2. Why does van den Haag believe that poor people are convicted of murder more often than wealthy people?
3. What does the author believe about guilt and justice?

Ernest van den Haag, "Murderers Deserve the Death Penalty." This article appeared in the November 1989 issue and is reprinted with permission from *The World & I*, a publication of The Washington Times Corporation, copyright © 1989.

According to polls, more than 70 percent of Americans feel that murderers deserve the death penalty. Innocents should never be punished, but the punishment for people who have committed crimes should be reasonably proportionate to their culpability and to the seriousness of their crimes. Hence, if a burglar deserves imprisonment, a murderer deserves death—the only punishment appropriate to his crime. Murderers do not deserve to survive their victims.

Currently the law in the 37 states [38 as of 1996] that have the death penalty provides that only those who have committed particularly heinous murders be sentenced to death. Usually, if a defendant is found guilty of murder, the jury, in a separate proceeding, is asked to determine whether the aggravating circumstances outweigh the mitigating ones (both listed in the law) and impose the death sentence only if that is the case. Thus, of the about 20,000 homicides committed annually in the United States, fewer than 300 lead to death sentences in any year. So far there have been on average 20 executions per year [in 1995 there were a record 56] (after an average waiting time of six to seven years)—too few to reduce the number of death row inmates (about 3,100 as of 1996), which continues to climb.

Nonetheless, the death penalty retains great symbolic and moral importance. It indicates strongly that each of us has a right to only one life—his own—and that he risks losing it if he takes someone else's. . . .

## The Advantages of Wealth

It is alleged that blacks and the poor often suffer the death penalty when equally guilty whites and wealthy people get away with murder. . . .

It is true that wealthy persons can afford a better legal defense than poor ones and thus may be able more readily to escape the death penalty. However, most murders are committed by poor persons, often during robberies. The wealthy rarely murder, just as they rarely commit burglaries, for obvious reasons. (They are more likely to commit "white-collar" crimes.)

No criminal justice system can totally avoid inequality despite all efforts to minimize it. Defendants are tried by different juries, judges, and lawyers—and even if they had the same amount of money to spend this would make a difference. All society can do is to make sure the defense attorneys are reasonably competent and that judges and juries are impartial. Even more important, of two persons guilty of murder, one may be found guilty and the other innocent if the first had the misfortune to have witnesses to the crime or other evidence against him and the second did not. Or one murderer may never be found, while the other is arrested immediately. We do not live in a perfect world.

Equal punishment for equal guilt is an ideal to strive for, but we should realize that it is not attainable. Systematic discrimination can be minimized—and great strides have been made in that direction—but accidental inequalities are hard to avoid. Unavoidably, some capriciousness and even some discrimination will remain in the system.

Reprinted by permission: Tribune Media Services.

Maldistribution often is used to argue that the death penalty should be abolished. Never mind, this argument goes, that these objections would apply to the penal system as a whole. Death is different. What is tolerable for imprisonment is not tolerable for capital punishment. Perhaps. But I don't see how discrimination or capriciousness make a death sentence unjust if the defendant is guilty.

### Guilt, Punishment, and Justice

Guilt is individual. If guilty whites or wealthy people escape the gallows and guilty poor people do not, the poor or black do not become less guilty because the others escaped their deserved punishment. Whether due to willful discrimination, capriciousness, or unavoidable accidental circumstances, some people will always get away with murder. Is that a reason to deny the justice of the punishment of those guilty persons who did not get away? Their guilt is not diminished by the escape of others, nor do they deserve less punishment because others did not get the punishment they deserve. Justice involves punishment according to what is deserved by the crime and the guilt of the criminal—regardless of whether others guilty of the same crime escape.

The death penalty is a deserved and just punishment for murder, and it is likely to deter some murders, thereby saving innocent lives. This possibility, as well as its justice, explains why more than two-thirds of all Americans favor capital punishment.

## 5

*"I have seen people with mental retardation . . . sitting in their own capital trials, with their lives at stake, who had absolutely no understanding of what was going on."*

# The Death Penalty Should Not Be Applied to the Retarded

Nat Hentoff

In 1989, in the case of *Penry v. Lynaugh*, the Supreme Court ruled that it is not cruel and unusual punishment to execute criminals who are mentally retarded. In the following viewpoint, Nat Hentoff describes the case of a mentally retarded man who was executed in Texas. Hentoff contends that such mentally retarded criminals are incapable of understanding the legal system, or even their own trials, and therefore they should be exempt from the death penalty. Hentoff is a columnist for the *Village Voice* and the *Washington Post*.

As you read, consider the following questions:

1. In Hentoff's opinion, what was the Supreme Court's rationale for the *Penry v. Lynaugh* ruling?
2. According to Ruth Luckasson, quoted by the author, what are the defining characteristics of mental retardation?

Nat Hentoff, "Executing the Retarded in Our Name," *Village Voice*, February 21, 1995. Reprinted by permission of the author.

*I remember very clearly the case of a mother watching her son with mental retardation standing trial for his life. One could see she had given a lot of thought to what she could do to comfort him, or to make some connection with this son who had such a low IQ. Finally, the one thing she found to do all day was to give him a small candy bar. That, at least, was something he could understand during his trial.*

—Ruth Luckasson

Mario Marquez, 36, was executed at 12:21 a.m. on January 17, 1995, by the state of Texas in Huntsville. Official killings have become so common there that—as a reporter for the *Huntsville Item* told *Nightline*—"The first few executions probably got people's attention, but you know when you get to 86 or 87, it just doesn't have the impact it used to."

And a resident of the death town added: "It's like you get up and eat breakfast every day. It's just something that happens that nobody pays attention to, I guess.". . .

### Marquez's Life and Crime

Mario Marquez's crime was horrible. As Ted Koppel said, "He raped and strangled a woman who was only 18, and a girl who was only a child of 14." The woman was his former wife, and the child was his niece.

What made this execution worthy of a front-page notice in the *Huntsville Item* was the debate over whether someone retarded should be executed. And that was one reason *Nightline* devoted two evenings to the last days of Mario Marquez.

A grade-school dropout with an IQ of 65, he was—as David Stout reported in the *New York Times*—"the 10th of 16 children born to a migrant farmworker and his wife. Repeatedly beaten with a horsewhip by his father, [Marquez was] then abandoned to the streets and a life of drug abuse when he was 12." Ted Koppel adds that he was "severely brain-damaged."

Marquez's lawyer, Robert McLassen, had worked on the case for five years. He is from the Texas Resource Center, and on *Nightline*, he told of a conversation with his client shortly before Marquez was no more: "Mario asked me tonight if he was going to have a good job when he goes to heaven. He wanted me to tell him whether I thought he could get a job being a gardener, or taking care of animals. I saw this young child up there."

Koppel reminded the lawyer of the two murders "this young child" had committed.

"I'm not saying," McLassen answered, "that someone who's mentally retarded like Mario shouldn't be punished for crimes like this, shouldn't be held accountable, in some sense. I just think it's fundamentally wrong to hold him as blameworthy as an adult."

What do you think? . . .

In Huntsville, Texas—which is becoming like the German towns near the gas chambers a half century ago—another resident says: "Since I've lived here all my life, I never even think about the prison or what's going on there. They—they just—it's all behind closed doors."

And yet another resident says calmly: "I really don't hear a whole lot about it from other people. We really—we really don't talk about it. I think it's just so, you know, normal here."

The big story in Texas on the day Mario Marquez left the state for good was the inauguration as governor of George W. Bush Jr., who said: "If we want our young Texans to learn to make correct choices, the consequences of bad behavior must be certain and must be clear."

To whom? Marquez had the mind of a seven-year-old.

---

## Retardation vs. Insanity

The barbarity of government-sanctioned killing takes on an extra foulness when the executed lack the intellectual capacity to understand either why they are caged year after year or why death awaits them at the end. The issue isn't guilt or innocence but guilt and its meaning. When courts focus on the mental condition of capital defendants, cases turn on insanity pleas. The mentally retarded are not insane, which is the mind having snapped. In retardation, a disability caused by a range of factors from fetal alcohol syndrome to genetic or biological disorders, the mind is present. It just isn't fully developed.

Colman McCarthy, *Liberal Opinion Week*, December 14, 1992.

---

Remember the old prison movies? When the electric chair began its work, the lights dimmed all over the prison and sometimes in the surrounding town. No one could escape a few moments' knowledge of the killing being done by the state in his or her name.

In Huntsville—the prison chaplain told Ted Koppel—before the coming of lethal injection, "when the switch was pulled, the lights all over town dimmed, so everybody had a feeling of when it was taking place."

But now, the residents of Texas, of other states with lethal injection, do not have to think about an execution when it takes place. And state killings are never shown on television, including *Nightline.* . . .

But what of the Supreme Court? Surely, when Texas executed the retarded Mario Marquez, it wasn't acting within clear Supreme Court precedent?

Well, there have been justices who would not vote for executing the retarded, but so far, they are in the minority. The determining Supreme Court decision in this macabre area is *Penry v. Lynaugh* (1989). By a five-to-four vote, the Court ruled that the Eighth Amendment ("cruel and unusual punishment") does not categorically prohibit the state from executing a mentally retarded person.

## The Supreme Court Ruling

Now dig this. The majority's rationale for allowing the killing of retarded murderers was that the High Court does not have "objective indicators" from society—that's us—to enable them to ban such executions.

"The clearest and most reliable objective evidence of contemporary values," said the victorious five justices, "are the laws passed by state legislatures and the actions of sentencing jurors."

The Court, therefore, largely based its ruling that retarded men and women can be executed on the basis of majority views around the nation. But the Eighth Amendment is part of the Bill of Rights, and that addition to the Constitution was clearly intended to protect the rights of *individuals* against the majority— including when the majority wants to kill defendants who are incapable of knowing what's going on.

In the *Penry* case, the majority opinion was written by that distinguished humanist Sandra Day O'Connor. The dissenters were, of course, William Brennan, Thurgood Marshall, Harry Blackmun, and John Paul Stevens.

An illustration of the kinds of state-court decisions that a majority of the Supreme Court used as support for its *Penry* opinion was shown in the 1989 Amnesty International book *When the State Kills: The death penalty, a human rights issue:*

"In January 1986, James Terry Roach was executed in South Carolina even though the trial judge had found him to be mentally retarded, and to be suffering from a personality disorder (later identified as the hereditary illness Huntington's chorea). . . . Furthermore, at 17, James Roach was a minor at the time of the crime."

A valuable Amnesty International paperback, *The Machinery of Death: A Shocking Indictment of Capital Punishment in the United States*, includes a chapter on the retarded and the death penalty.

Professor Ruth Luckasson makes two key points in her first paragraph:

"Many individuals who are sentenced to death and executed in this country have mental retardation. Mental retardation is a mental disability distinct from mental illness. Frequently there is a confusion about the two disabilities in the judicial system

174

and among citizens of this country."

The defining characteristics of mental retardation are: "significantly subaverage intellectual functioning, accompanying impairments in the adaptive skills of the person, and manifestation of the disability before the age of 18. It is, by definition, a very serious liability that affects every dimension of a person's life."

Nonetheless, "there are adults in the criminal justice system who have mental ages of six, seven, and eight."

Mario Marquez, for instance. Except that he's no longer in the criminal justice system.

### The Retarded Don't Understand the System

By contrast with some forms of mental illness, which are hard to evaluate, mental retardation "is relatively easy to document and evaluate. Almost uniformly, individuals with mental retardation have grave difficulties in language and communication . . . attention, memory, intellectual rigidity and moral development or moral understanding. They are very susceptible to suggestion . . . and have serious problems in logic, planning and understanding consequences."

As Professor Luckasson emphasizes, "Can you imagine anyone easier to execute?" Particularly since "defendants with mental retardation do not get thorough evaluation. . . . Their limitations are ignored, interpreted away, or used to unjustly convict them. Good investigations are not conducted in these cases, so even what should be the routine collection of an individual's school and medical records is not done. . . .

"Police officers, judges, prosecutors and even the clients' own lawyers fail to pick up on the mental retardation. . . . *Consider each step of a capital proceeding, and superimpose on each step significantly impaired intelligence. You will have some idea of why a person with mental retardation, once caught in the system, cannot escape."* (Emphasis added.)

She tells of a mentally retarded man in Texas who was executed in 1992. He had given an incriminating statement to the police after they had put their guns on the table and told him, "I tell you what, nigger, I'll gun you down on the spot."

The retarded man had signed his own death warrant and he was moved briskly through the judicial system.

In this nation—where schoolchildren every morning pledge allegiance "to the flag of the United States of America and to the republic for which it stands, one nation under God, indivisible, with liberty and justice for all"—this is American justice:

"I have seen people with mental retardation," says Ruth Luckasson, "sitting in their own capital trials, with their lives at stake, who had absolutely no understanding of what was going on."

## 6

"If a person commits a uniquely gruesome
murder, he deserves to be put to death."

# The Retarded Should
# Not Be Exempt
# from the Death Penalty

Chris Gersten

In January 1995, Mario Marquez was executed in Texas even
though his lawyers claimed he was mentally retarded. In the
following viewpoint, Chris Gersten argues that capital punishment is reserved for the worst murderers, and Marquez's crime
was so brutal that it warranted his execution despite his low IQ.
Americans strongly support the death penalty, Gersten contends, and they should continue to demand capital punishment
for such vicious killers. Gersten is the director of the Center for
Jewish and Christian Values in Washington, D.C.

As you read, consider the following questions:

1. According to Gersten, how long did the jury deliberate in
   Marquez's case?
2. In the author's words, what was Marquez's last clemency
   appeal based on?
3. What aggravating factors must be present for a murderer to
   be sentenced to death, according to the author?

Chris Gersten, "He Was Such a Nice Murderer, Too," *Washington Times*, January 20, 1995.
Reprinted by permission of the author.

On January 27, 1984, Mario Marquez, twenty-six years old, a convicted burglar out on bond, was about to be divorced by his eighteen-year-old wife, Rebecca. He wanted to get even with her, so he went to the home where his wife and sister-in-law, Rosa Gutierrez, were staying and methodically sodomized and strangled his wife and his niece, Rachael Gutierrez, fourteen. Marquez bit his victims while raping them. After murdering the two women he waited for his wife's sister, Rosa, to come home. He took Rosa upstairs so she could see her dead daughter and sister. Then he sodomized her.

Marquez was convicted of killing his niece. He was charged but not tried for killing his wife. The prosecuting attorney, Sam Millsap, called the slayings the most brutal he had seen. After four hours of deliberation, a jury found Marquez guilty and later sentenced him to die by lethal injection.

After more than ten years of appeals, Marquez was executed early Tuesday morning, January 17, 1995. It was the 87th execution since Texas reinstated the death penalty in 1982.

## Apathy Toward Those Executed?

Ted Koppel devoted two editions of *Nightline* to capital punishment. He aired the show from the Huntsville Prison in Texas, with a focus on the case of Mario Marquez. Mr. Koppel said, "The point will not be to debate the merit of capital punishment": only that we must not be "apathetic" when we execute someone. Mr. Koppel continued, "The more we as a nation support the death penalty, the less interested we are in those who are executed in our name."

But, without saying capital punishment is immoral, Mr. Koppel did everything he could to make the viewer feel that executing Marquez was wrong. Mr. Koppel did not say one word about the crime. He did not mention that Marquez was charged with a double murder, killing his wife as well as his niece, until late in the second show, and then, only in passing. He did not tell the audience that Marquez sodomized and bit his victims before strangling them. And Mr. Koppel did not tell his audience that only particularly vicious killings ever result in the death penalty. Mr. Koppel did not interview Rosa Gutierrez, the mother and sister of the victims. He did not interview any family members to ask what they thought Marquez's punishment should be.

Mr. Koppel began by interviewing another death-row inmate, Jesse Jacobs, before Marquez was executed. He asked the felon if he thought the death penalty served as a deterrent to murder. Jacobs replied, "Kids on the streets, they say, 'Well, the state's killing people every day, . . . and we can do it too. You can't tell me I can't do something when you do it and get away with it.' Is it a deterrent? No."

177

A local resident said, "Texas executes more than anyone, but crime is still on the rise, so it must not be working."

Then Mr. Koppel interviewed the chaplain, Carroll Pickett, who spends the final hours with each Texas convict about to be executed. Mr. Koppel asked the chaplain if he could sleep at night after the executions. And, of course, the answer was no.

---

## Mental Retardation and the Death Penalty

Some contend that laws protecting the mentally retarded from the death penalty open the way for any inmate with even slightly below-average intelligence to use his or her mental capacity as an excuse for murder. In a case in Arkansas, convicted murderer Barry Lee Fairchild, 41, was denied clemency, even after his lawyers charged that he was mentally retarded. According to his lawyer, Fairchild had an I.Q. of 60 to 80, "depending on who gives the test and when." (I.Q. stands for intelligence quotient, a test used to measure general knowledge and comprehension. A normal I.Q. is 100.)

Although Arkansas law forbids the execution of defendants with an I.Q. of 65 or lower, Judge Thomas Eisele said there was insufficient evidence that Fairchild had such a low mental capacity. Fairchild was executed by lethal injection on August 31, 1995.

*Issues and Controversies on File*, December 29, 1995.

---

Mr. Koppel interviewed Marquez's attorney, Robert McLasson, who tried to stay the execution. The entire appeal was based on the fact that Marquez's IQ was purportedly only 65, making him retarded and therefore unable to know right from wrong.

After the execution, Mr. McLasson says, "I am damaged, I think this damages us all. This was an inhumane thing."

And Mr. Koppel interviewed Marquez himself. After ten years on death row, Marquez had mellowed more than a little. He was a sympathetic character, speaking in English with a thick Spanish accent. He certainly didn't sound retarded. Marquez said he was ready to die.

Mr. Koppel described the family of the killer. During the execution, the brothers wept and the mother said her rosary, a few blocks away. Again, not a word about the families of the victims.

### Anything but Apathy

We are left to feel that somehow executing such a pathetic figure with a low IQ makes the executioner the villain. And, implied by Mr. Koppel, all of us are guilty because we are "apathetic" about capital punishment.

Another local resident says, "It's just something that happens. No one pays attention anymore."

But we are anything but apathetic about the death penalty. Fully 80 percent of the public supports the death penalty, according to recent polls. And Texas, which has executed the most people since 1982, is the least apathetic. Texans, like most other Americans, believe that if a person commits a uniquely gruesome murder, he deserves to be put to death.

What Mr. Koppel so pointedly refused to tell his audience was that the Marquez crime was an unusually sadistic double murder. Run-of-the-mill murders almost never get the death penalty. There must be aggravating factors such as multiple murders or mutilation or torture for a murderer to be sentenced to death.

In fact, the average sentence for murder in this country is a little over fifteen years. And the average time served is just five and a half years, according to the FBI.

But Mr. Koppel did not share that information either. By turning the killer and his family into the victims and keeping the real victims and their families completely out of the picture, Mr. Koppel attempted to make us sympathize with the killer. If we identify with the killer, then to put him to death must be wrong. That is what Mr. Koppel seems to believe. The American people disagree.

# Periodical Bibliography

The following articles have been selected to supplement the diverse views presented in this chapter. Addresses are provided for periodicals not indexed in the *Readers' Guide to Periodical Literature*, the *Alternative Press Index*, or the *Social Sciences Index*.

| | |
|---|---|
| William F. Buckley | "The Susan Smith Case," *National Review*, August 28, 1995. |
| J. Daryl Charles | "Justice by Quota," *National Review*, September 12, 1994. |
| Talbot D'Alemberte | "Racial Injustice and American Justice," *ABA Journal*, August 1992. Available from 750 N. Lake Shore Dr., Chicago, IL 60611. |
| Martin Garbus | "Executioners' Song," *Nation*, December 19, 1994. |
| Ted Gest | "Crime's Bias Problem," *U.S. News & World Report*, July 25, 1994. |
| Stanley Holmes | "The Tortuous Tale of a Serial Killer," *Newsweek*, April 25, 1994. |
| Julie Johnson | "Numbering Their Days," *Time*, May 23, 1994. |
| Peter Linebaugh | "The Farce of the Death Penalty," *Nation*, August 14–21, 1995. |
| Mari Matsuda | "Crime and Punishment," *Ms.*, November/December 1994. |
| *National Review* | "John Conyers's Root Causes," May 16, 1994. |
| *National Review* | "Justice for Medea," August 28, 1995. |
| *New Republic* | "He Shot the Sheriff," September 4, 1995. |
| Tina Rosenberg | "The Deadliest D.A.," *New York Times Magazine*, July 16, 1995. |
| Tina Rosenberg | "On the Row," *Rolling Stone*, October 5, 1995. |
| Jill Smolowe | "Mumia on Their Mind," *Time*, August 6, 1995. |
| Jill Smolowe | "Untrue Confessions," *Time*, May 22, 1995. |
| Kathryn V. Stanley | "An Eye for an Eye?" *Essence*, December 1994. |
| Susan D. Strater | "The Juvenile Death Penalty: In the Best Interests of the Child?" *Human Rights*, Spring 1995. Available from 750 N. Lake Shore Dr., Chicago, IL 60611. |

# For Further Discussion

## Chapter 1

1. The author of the first viewpoint argues that for criminals who "have no expectations beyond the Grave," only capital punishment will serve as a deterrent. In Cesare Beccaria's view, why is long-term imprisonment a more effective deterrent to criminals than death? Which author do you find more persuasive, and why?

2. Horace Greeley contends that capital punishment "weakens the natural horror of bloodshed" and teaches disregard for human life. How does John Stuart Mill counter this argument? In Mill's opinion, what does the death penalty teach about human life?

3. Robert E. Crowe maintains that criminals often commit murder in the course of robberies "on the theory that dead men can make no identifications." In Clarence Darrow's opinion, why do burglars often kill their victims? What does Darrow think is the cause of criminal behavior? How does his view contrast with Crowe's?

## Chapter 2

1. Charles W. Colson argues that the purpose of capital punishment is to enforce social order and maintain society's sense of justice. In Helen Prejean's view, why is the death penalty counterproductive to these purposes in modern society? What modern social movements does she cite? What lessons does she draw from these movements?

2. Harry A. Blackmun contends that capital punishment should be abolished because there is an irreconcilable conflict between the constitutional principles of applying the death penalty fairly and applying it consistently. In Antonin Scalia's opinion, how should this conflict be resolved? According to Scalia, what should be the overriding factor in resolving the conflict? Which argument do you find more persuasive, and why?

3. Michael L. Radelet, Hugo Adam Bedau, and Constance E. Putnam argue that the likelihood that innocent people will be convicted and executed should preclude the use of the death penalty. Do you agree with this argument? Why or why not? Do you find their evidence of innocent people having been executed convincing? Defend your answer using examples from the text.

# Chapter 3

1. Richard L. Nygaard maintains that imprisonment deters murderers as effectively as the death penalty does. How does John J. DiIulio Jr. counter this argument? What evidence does he provide to support his view? In your opinion, which author provides the more convincing evidence? Explain.

2. Wendy Kaminer contends that the writ of habeas corpus enshrines the right to federal judicial review of criminal convictions and sentences. In her opinion, why is a lengthy process of review necessary for justice? In the view of Arlen Specter, why would a lengthy review result in a miscarriage of justice?

3. According to Michael Ross, how much more expensive are capital trials than noncapital ones? Under what circumstances are the added costs valid, according to Alex Kozinski and Sean Gallagher? Which argument do you find more persuasive? Cite examples from the viewpoints to defend your opinion.

# Chapter 4

1. Michael Ross presents statistics showing that the death penalty is applied disproportionately to blacks, particularly when their victims are white. How do Stanley Rothman and Stephen Powers explain this phenomenon? Do you find their explanation convincing? Why or why not?

2. Nick DiSpoldo charges that the death penalty is applied unfairly to the poor because they cannot afford the same kind of legal defense that the wealthy can. In Ernest van den Haag's opinion, why are the poor more likely than the rich to receive death sentences? According to van den Haag, what other factors cause disparities in sentences? Which argument do you find more persuasive, and why?

3. According to Nat Hentoff, why should mentally retarded defendants be exempt from the death penalty? How should they be punished, in his opinion? How do you think Chris Gersten would respond to these arguments? Defend your answer using examples from the text.

# Organizations to Contact

The editors have compiled the following list of organizations concerned with the issues debated in this book. The descriptions are derived from materials provided by the organizations. All have publications or information available for interested readers. The list was compiled on the date of publication of the present volume; names, addresses, phone numbers, and fax numbers may change. Be aware that many organizations take several weeks or longer to respond to inquiries, so allow as much time as possible.

**Capital Punishment Project**
American Civil Liberties Union (ACLU)
122 Maryland Ave. NE
Washington, DC 20002
(202) 675-2321

The project is dedicated to abolishing the death penalty. The ACLU believes that capital punishment violates the Constitution's ban on cruel and unusual punishment as well as the requirements of due process and equal protection under the law. It publishes and distributes numerous books and pamphlets, including *The Case Against the Death Penalty* and *Frequently Asked Questions Concerning the Writ of Habeas Corpus and the Death Penalty.*

**Death Penalty Information Center (DPIC)**
1606 20th St. NW, 2nd Fl.
Washington, DC 20009
(202) 347-2531

DPIC conducts research into public opinion on the death penalty. The center opposes capital punishment because it is discriminatory, excessively costly, and may result in the execution of innocent persons. It publishes numerous reports, such as *Millions Misspent: What Politicians Don't Say About the High Costs of the Death Penalty, Innocence and the Death Penalty: Assessing the Danger of Mistaken Executions,* and *With Justice for Few: The Growing Crisis in Death Penalty Representation.*

**Justice Fellowship**
PO Box 16069
Washington, DC 20041-6069
(703) 904-7312

This Christian organization bases its work for reform of the justice system on the concept of victim-offender reconciliation. It does not take a position on the death penalty, but it publishes the pamphlet *Capital Punishment: A Call to Dialogue.*

**Justice Now**
PO Box 62132
North Charleston, SC 29419-2132

This organization supports the death penalty as a solution to the problems of crime and overcrowded prisons in the United States. It maintains information resources, which it makes available to the public, consisting of books, pamphlets, periodicals, newspaper clippings, and bibliographies on the subjects of serial killers, death row prisoners, executions, prisons, and courts.

## Lamp of Hope Project
13931 N. Central Expressway, #246
Dallas, TX 75243

The project was established and is primarily run by Texas death row inmates. It works for victim-offender reconciliation and for the protection of the civil rights of prisoners, particularly the right of habeas corpus appeal. It publishes and distributes the periodic *Texas Death Row Journal*.

## Lincoln Institute for Research and Education
1001 Connecticut Ave. NW
Washington, DC 20036
(202) 223-5112

The institute is a conservative think tank that studies public policy issues affecting the lives of black Americans, including the issue of the death penalty, which it favors. It publishes the quarterly *Lincoln Review*.

## NAACP Legal Defense and Education Fund
99 Hudson St., Suite 1600
New York, NY 10013-2897
(212) 219-1900

Founded by the National Association for the Advancement of Colored People, the fund opposes the death penalty and works to end discrimination in the justice system. It compiles and reports statistics on the death penalty and publishes legal materials, fact sheets, and reports.

## National Criminal Justice Reference Service (NCJRS)
U.S. Department of Justice
Box 6000
Rockville, MD 20850
(800) 851-3420

For a nominal fee, the NCJRS provides topical searches and reading lists on many areas of criminal justice, including the death penalty.

## National Legal Aid & Defender Association (NLADA)
1625 K St. NW, 8th Fl.
Washington, DC 20006
(202) 452-0620

NLADA provides technical assistance to and acts as a clearinghouse for organizations that provide legal aid services to the poor. It advocates high-quality legal services for the indigent. The association publishes materials to assist legal-services organizations and distributes reports by death penalty opponents.

# Bibliography of Books

| | |
|---|---|
| Mumia Abu-Jamal | *Live from Death Row.* Reading, MA: Addison-Wesley, 1995. |
| Robert M. Baird and Stuart E. Rosenbaum | *Punishment and the Death Penalty: The Current Debate.* Amherst, NY: Prometheus Books, 1995. |
| Walter Berns | *For Capital Punishment: Crime and the Morality of the Death Penalty.* Lanham, MD: University Press of America, 1991. |
| Mark Brandler | *The Death Penalty—View from the Bench: An Autobiography.* New York: Vantage, 1993. |
| Committee on the Judiciary | *Innocence and the Death Penalty: Assessing the Danger of Mistaken Executions.* Washington, DC: Government Printing Office, 1994. |
| Randall Coyne and Lyn Entzeroth | *Capital Punishment and the Judicial Process.* Durham, NC: Carolina Academic Press, 1994. |
| Shirley Dicks | *Young Blood: Juvenile Justice and the Death Penalty.* Amherst, NY: Prometheus Books, 1995. |
| Richard C. Dieter | *The Future of the Death Penalty in the United States: A Texas-Sized Crisis.* Washington, DC: Death Penalty Information Center, 1994. |
| Gary E. Goldhammer | *Dead End.* Brunswick, ME: Briddle, 1994. |
| Enid Harlow et al., eds. | *The Machinery of Death: A Shocking Indictment of Capital Punishment in the United States.* New York: Amnesty International, 1995. |
| Wendy Lesser | *Pictures at an Execution.* Cambridge, MA: Harvard University Press, 1993. |
| James W. Marquart et al. | *The Rope, the Chair, and the Needle: Capital Punishment in Texas, 1923–1990.* Austin: University of Texas Press, 1994. |
| Kent S. Miller | *Executing the Mentally Ill: The Criminal Justice System and the Case of Alvin Ford.* Newbury Park, CA: Sage Publications, 1993. |
| Raymond Paternoster | *Capital Punishment in America.* New York: Lexington Books, 1991. |
| Emily F. Reed | *The Penry Penalty: Capital Punishment and Offenders with Mental Retardation.* Lanham, MD: University Press of America, 1993. |
| Eric W. Rise | *The Martinville Seven: Race, Rape, and Capital Punishment.* Charlottesville: University Press of Virginia, 1995. |

Gregory D. Russell     *The Death Penalty and Racial Bias: Overturning Supreme Court Assumptions.* Westport, CT: Greenwood Press, 1994.

William Schaba     *The Abolition of the Death Penalty in International Law.* Cambridge: Grotius Publications, 1993.

Stephen Trombley     *The Execution Protocol: Inside America's Capital Punishment Industry.* New York: Crown, 1992.

Mark V. Tushnet     *The Death Penalty.* New York: Facts On File, 1994.

David Von Drehle     *Among the Lowest of the Dead: A Decade on Death Row.* New York: Times Books, 1995.

# Index

187

190